Masters of the Links

edited by
Geoff Shackelford

SLEEPING BEAR PRESS

Library of Congress Cataloging-in-Publiscation Data
Masters of the links / edited by Geoff D. Shackelford.
p. cm.
ISBN 1-886947-27-9
1. Golf courses--Design and construction. 2. Golf courses--Maintenance and repair. I. Shackelford, Geoff D.
GV975.M337 1997
796.352'06'8--dc21

Sleeping Bear Press
121 South Main
P.O. Box 20
Chelsea, MI 48118

Sleeping Bear Ltd.
7 Medallion Place
Maidenhead, Berkshire
England

Printed and bound in Canada by Friesen's, Altona, Manitoba.

10 9 8 7 6 5 4 3 2 1

Front cover painting of "Summer Clear Day, 7th at Pebble Beach, circa 1929" by Mike Miller. Pebble Beach, Pebble Beach Golf Links, and distinctive images of its golf course and golf hole designs, are trademarks, service marks and trade dress of Pebble Beach Company, reproduced by permission.

Contents

Part III—Planning, Construction, and Maintenance

Part IV—Hazards and Holes

Part V—Contemporary Design

Acknowledgments

Many thanks to all of those who helped with the research and information contained inside this book: Saundra Sheffer, Marge Dewey, Sid Matthew, Daniel Wexler, George Bahto, John Strawn, Scot Sherman, James Brewer, and Jim Snow.

A special appreciation to three people who left us some time ago but whose work through the Ralph W. Miller Golf Library resulted in an amazing collection of books, photographs, and magazines. First, a thank you to Ralph W. Miller, a long-time Southern California attorney and golf enthusiast who clipped, read, and saved countless articles, not to mention accumulated so many remarkable books. And to Bill and Jean Bryant, who were instrumental in the City of Industry's acquisition of Mr. Miller's collection and who added so much to it over the years—your dedication will always be cherished.

Immense gratitude is extended to those who have been instrumental in my golf architecture education and in seeing this book to its fruition: Ben Crenshaw, Bill Coore, Bradley Klein, Tom Doak, Dan Proctor, Dave Axland, Gil Hanse, and Ron Forse. And to Mr. and Mrs. Dye, thank you for your interesting essays in this book and for making such important contributions to golf architecture. Your devotion to the game and training of so many fine architects are truly remarkable gifts to golf architecture.

Many thanks to those in Los Angeles who have been supportive: my parents Lynn and Diane, Ron Papell, Mike Riedel, Eric Shortz, and Bob William. Also, my gratitude to Mike Miller and Alex Galvan, whose art work has added so much to this book and to my previous effort, *The Captain*.

Finally, a special thank you to Ron Whitten and Geoffrey Cornish, whose groundbreaking volume, *The Architects of Golf*, opened all of our eyes to the wonders of golf architecture and made books like this one possible.

Introduction

When my last book was published, I carried an enormous sense of pride because I believed the book answered many questions about George C. Thomas Jr. and brought his work to the attention of a new generation. Captain Thomas had been dead for over 60 years, but I felt his many fine contributions to golf architecture might now be enjoyed by those who appreciate such things.

One day, after the book had been out for a while, the Green Committee Chairman at my club invited me to play golf at a course originally designed by Thomas. We were paired up with a member of this particular club's Green Committee, and as we strolled down the first fairway, this other gentleman in our group asked what I did for a living. I replied by telling him of my new book on George Thomas, called *The Captain*. To which he proudly exclaimed, "Oh, why he was just here last week!"

Needless to say, I spent the rest of the day thinking about what my next book would be since it was clear that another effort was needed to celebrate and preserve the work of the master golf architects from Captain Thomas' era.

The Captain opened with a quote from Bobby Jones, which despite my efforts to find something a bit more current, is still the best thing anyone has ever said about why golfers should want to learn about golf course architecture:

> Every golfer worthy of the name should have some acquaintance with the principles of golf course design, not only for the betterment of the game, but for his own selfish enjoyment. Let him know a good hole from a bad one and the reasons for a bunker here and another there, and he will be a long way towards pulling his score down to respectable limits. When he has taught himself to study a hole from the point of view of the man who laid it out, he will be much more likely to play it correctly.

In this day when the simplest sound bytes will elect a President or get golf architects the most prestigious contracts, Mr. Jones' dialogue on "every golfer worthy of the name" summarizes the essence of this book.

Golf is a complex game with many fascinating components, yet none is more distinct than the architecture of its courses. When golf course design was celebrating its finest hour, 1933, Mr. Jones was asking golfers to pay more attention to architecture not only for the betterment of golf but to enhance their own games. Jones knew that if golfers had some understanding of golf architecture principles, they would better enjoy their courses and likely shoot lower scores. Whether you are playing one of the great layouts in the world or the most ordinary municipal track, a round of golf will be much more enjoyable by having some knowledge of course design.

Golf architecture is an art form, and, as with other art forms, the more you learn about the thought (or in many cases, lack of thought) put into the design, the more you will appreciate playing a well-designed course. Once the golfer begins to understand the principles of golf architecture, not only is he or she likely to play a well-conceived course more successfully, but that player will also be able to recognize a poorly designed hole—an ability that can prove to be perversely satisfying. Once a player achieves even a rudimentary understanding of golf course architecture, this most interesting of games becomes that much more appealing.

The best golf courses always have extraordinary diversity integrated into their design. Whether it be in the form of short holes, long holes, tee shots that require fades, tee shots that call for a forced carry, small and flat greens, and large, undulating putting surfaces, the possibilities are endless.

As with any commendable music collection or fine art portfolio, the goal of *Masters of the Links* is to provide the reader with a *variety* of subjects by a medley of architects. Several of the greatest architects of all time are featured in this book: C.B. Macdonald, Alister MacKenzie, and A.W. Tillinghast are the fathers of American golf architecture, and their work has proved to be the most enduring.

Some very talented, but not as well-known designers are also included: William Flynn, George Thomas, Robert Hunter, and William Langford. Their designs were in harmony with those of "the founding fathers" and each left a remarkable legacy to golf. For more variety, Bobby Jones, the greatest amateur golfer of all time, is included as are two of history's most engaging and knowledgeable golf writers: O.B. Keeler and Bernard Darwin.

For the first time in decades, a collection of essays is included from contemporary figures in golf architecture. Some you may have heard of, like Pete Dye, Tom Doak, or Ben Crenshaw. Others may not be familiar to you, but each was selected due to their respect for the "master" architects listed above and because their wisdom will add to your enjoyment and comprehension of golf course design.

The old articles compiled for this book have been virtually "lost" for the last 60 years. Most were found in obscure golf publications or from the two major golf magazines of the "Golden Age" of golf design: *The American Golfer* and *Golf Illustrated.* The essays have been reproduced here basically as they appeared when published. When possible, the original art work and photography have been included, with several additions. In only a few cases were essays edited, usually to eliminate text concerning problems with extinct golf balls or outdated agronomic issues which might detract from the more relevant points.

Masters of the Links is designed so that the novice student of golf architecture can become acquainted with the subject, while there is plenty of new material to enrich the advanced students' library. There is a glossary in the Appendix that should help with some of the more unfamiliar terms used in the essays, and a bibliography is published for those desiring reference tools.

Since the departure of the many "master architects," post-1930s golf architecture has become remarkably stale. The average golfer's expectations have been lowered because of a lack of available information on the subject and more sadly, a lack of access to well-designed, affordable courses. I hope this book, along with the other architecture-related publications of late, will encourage golfers to demand a level of golf architecture comparable to the sophistication it once enjoyed when the "masters" were at work.

Geoff Shackelford
April 1997

Masters of the Links

~

Every opportunity is provided on the Old Course for bringing out the essentials of great golf. St. Andrews is difficult, not because bunkers are placed to catch inaccurate shots, but because the result of a misadventure is to make the next shot infinitely more difficult than it would otherwise have been. No shot can ever be said to be easy on this most subtle of all courses so long as the surface is keen and slippery. Nor on this classic course is there ever any one absolute way open to the hole. To choose a line of play is, as not, very much a choice of evils. Each successive shot must be played on its own merits. The subtle folds in the ground short of the greens govern for the most part—especially when the going is fast—the final result, and unusual finesse is needed if the run of the ball is to be accurately judged. For these amongst other reasons St. Andrews is the ideal to aim at in all golf-course construction.

—H.N. Wethered and Tom Simpson

~

PART I

St. Andrews and Links

The goal of Part I is to explore the Old Course at St. Andrews and discover how it has shaped the game, and in particular, its influence on the architects responsible for our best courses. Virtually all of the most enduring golf course design traits have been derived from the Old Course, and today it stands as more than a historic landmark to the game of golf—it is still one of the world's finest tests of skill.

Part I presents Robert Hunter's eloquent prescription for his ideal course while Alister MacKenzie provides his typical straightforward wit in "Pleasurable Golf Courses." Finally, O.B. Keeler shares what he watched and overheard during a 1926 visit to the British Isles with Bobby Jones.

~

Editor's Note
Robert Hunter and His Ideal Course

Every devoted golfer is an architect in his own mind. And we have all imagined what our ideal course looks like. We have designed it in our heads and in moments of true boredom, have planned our ideal course down to the very last detail. In "The Ideal Golf Course," Robert Hunter gives us his prerequisites for a dream course, tells us about an existing layout that he has in mind as an ideal, and even goes so far as to specify where it would sit in relation to his garden! But why should we care what Mr. Hunter's dream course would look like?

Robert Hunter was one of the most fascinating characters in early twentieth century golf architecture, despite never having designed a golf course on his own. He wrote one of golf's most brilliant architecture books, *The Links*, but his actual design work in the field was limited to assisting Dr. Alister MacKenzie on such noted courses as Cypress Point Club, The Meadow Club, and The Valley Club of Montecito—all in California.

An Indiana native, Hunter's name is also attributed to some minor redesign work at Monterey Peninsula Country Club's underrated Dunes Course and he aided H. Chandler Egan in remodeling Pebble Beach Golf Links for the 1929 U.S. Amateur. Hunter was primarily responsible for luring MacKenzie to California, and the two formed a brief design partnership with Egan, the two-time U.S. Amateur Champion.

The depth of Robert Hunter's writing on golf and design in *The Links*, and in the following article, reveals a profound man whose fantasies about an ideal course are sure to be worth your while.

G.S.

~

The Ideal Golf Course

by Robert Hunter

The American Golfer
January 1927

In writing of the ideal golf course one must assume, for instance, that for the lover of this sport the ideal course will never lose its charm; that it will always present to him interesting problems; and that his delight in it will increase no matter how often nor for how many years he plays it. We must assume that it will test and discipline him in the slashing days of his youth; that it will thrill and defy him in the days of his mastery; and that it will still afford him real pleasure to the last green on the last day. This is much, but we are thinking of the ideal golf course.

It must certainly be a course which the champions will respect and this cannot be unless it is to call forth their finest effort. It must be a real test of their skill and if there be a weakness in their repertoire of strokes it shall uncover their short-comings. On the other hand it must give enjoyment to those of lesser skill and of minor talent; and above all it must awaken interest in the youth and lead him to develop the best that is in him. It will indeed reward power; but only when that power is controlled and precisely used.

The ideal course shall be all this and yet more. It will regard those of limited strength and those whose vigor is passing. For these latter, it will always hold out the joyous opportunity to play those more cultivated strokes which years of training on the green have refined and which do not depend upon mere power. I know well two great champions of earlier years who cannot now always carry a hazard one hundred yards from the tee, but who still play the game and have shots in their bag which Hagen and Jones would view with envy. On my ideal course these shall not be denied nor yet humiliated.

My ideal course shall be on comparatively flat sandy soil amongst little hillocks and hollows and preferably by the sea. It shall lie at the border of my garden or, if it must be, down a very short lane. It should have—though this is too much to ask and is not essential—the sunny, even climate and glorious view of mountains and of sea such as we have here at Pebble Beach. And yet while this most satisfying course calls for fine golf, it is not my ideal, although it is surely the most beautiful in the world.

The one so much desired shall be clothed in a fine velvety turf and that of the greens shall hardly be distinguished from that of the tees and fairways. Indeed it shall be difficult to define where the greens begin and the fairways end. Tees and greens shall be very like the country all about except that near the hole we shall find many subtle hollows and slopes besprinkled here and there with sandy depressions. There shall be no obvious erections or ridges, no embankments and terraces, but the ground shall be sculptured in gentle, flowing lines as if the wind had played upon it and tumbled it about before the turf had bound it down.

Throughout the fairways, there shall be other hazards but these shall be scattered about devoid of apparent plan; some of them lying where good shots are likely to go. One or two shall indeed lie just where one would most like to place his tee-shots.

This will mean that from the tee and from the lie, one shall be required to play with skill and circumspection. If one cannot carry the hazard, one must play to the right or the left. The long hitter, who aspires to be a champion, must face, as he should wish to do, the severest hazards and place his ball on the narrowest bit of fairway; and when by his length or wildness he appears to have escaped all penalties, he shall yet have to consider, in his battle with Par, a green with treacherous slopes and with hazards which snuggle up close to the pin.

There shall be all manner of good holes on my course and no two of them shall be alike. There shall be greens of many varieties; some quite large, others very small. They shall have mild hummocks and hollows and other delightful undulations upon and about them; because when I grow very old, I shall still wish to toddle down the lane and have my hour of delight. To some of the little harbors where the flag flies there shall be narrow and hazardous channels and here all manner of fine, precise shots shall be called for. Some will have to be played low, some quite high and some must run for a long way, while others must stop short. There shall be no compulsory carries from the tee unless one insists upon going bang for the pin and then often heroic things shall be asked of daring ones. Length will be necessary for those who try to belittle Par and we shall have it even if we must build back tees to draw the "tigers" out and give them their seven thousand yards; but he to whom length is denied shall always have his forward tees and his route to the hole if he will but play it.

Few would be bold enough to sketch too precisely an ideal course of the type I have briefly outlined and it would be brash to start a controversy upon such lines among the habitués of any club. The mere thought of such a discussion is a bit terrifying and I can almost hear the derisive laughter and the "Impossible!", "Ridiculous!", "Silly dreamer!", and other such comments. But what I may hesitate to discuss face to face, because I should never be heard to the finish, I shall write. The thing has been done. I know at least one such course by Donald Ross, one by Walter Travis, and several by Dr. MacKenzie: but as you, doubting reader, may not know these courses, I shall not bring them into the argument. But I shall mention one, and this will, I think, be conclusive. The greatest course in the world is almost all that I have here described! The Old Course at St. Andrews is the one I have in mind, and if it lacks in any point, it is not an essential one.

Where else in the world do we find a course to which all great players journey and where all ages and abilities meet and all praise with equal fervor? What other course can we all name which defies the champions and yet delights tottering old age? What other course can be played with a putter—the Swilken Burn being in that case the only serious obstacle—and at the same time be spoken of, by those qualified to speak, as the best course in the world? Is not this very nearly the thought of Ouimet, Gardner and Jones? To my mind, and to that of far more competent judges, St. Andrews is so near to the ideal that one would be most ungrateful to seek further for anything more perfect in this most imperfect world.

Every time I visit St. Andrews my love and admiration for it increases. I should rather play that course for the rest of my life than any other I know. I should never grow weary of it; nor should I ever conquer it; and every round would whet my appetite to tackle it again on the morrow. Bobby Jones last summer gracefully acknowledged its difficulties. He did not hesitate to admit that on every round he was faced with something new, and that a score of from 72 to 75 was not despised; and while this is praise indeed, only the old boys know how really great the Old Course is. There have been champions who could never master its problems—Harry Vardon, strange to say, was one of them—and to them and others it will always remain a mystery.

One must take time to know the Old Course in all its moods. One must study the subtleties of its terrain and its curiously shifting winds. One must find its hidden snares and one must approach it without preconceptions of what a golf course should be. To be down the middle may mean nothing there; that may be quite the wrong place. To be long may mean nothing unless length is shrewdly used. To be able to play a few shots perfectly is not always enough; one must at times have the full repertoire. Bernard Darwin is a thoughtful understanding golfer but even he had to visit St. Andrews many times before falling victim to its charms and greatness. Others may never see them, Jesse Guilford for instance. I can yet see that sturdy lad, as he played his Walker Cup matches, wandering about the course in a profound mental fog, cursing like the proverbial pirate and berating the course as the one worst in all the world. It was beating him as it has beaten many other great golfers, used in their high manner to despise hazards, even such magnificent hazards as those of Pine Valley, which may be conquered by power.

St. Andrews yields nothing to power unless it be used with wisdom. There it, too, must be disciplined and refined. Like all other courses St. Andrews has its vulnerable spots, but they must be struck. Let one be a little off center and all one's most powerful blows fall futile. One must hit to position. One must open up the hole. One must consider the slope of the green.

One must place himself in position to attack it. One may in certain positions be better off a hundred yards from the green than in the wrong position at its very edge. That bewhiskered old timer there hitting to position, rolling his ball almost along the ground, may do his round in the eighties; while siege guns boom in vain and youthful champions with their prodigious power return from a campaign they have never wholly understood with a score which sickens them.

If one were to pick certain holes to illustrate what is meant by the ideal, I should place first of all the fourteenth at St. Andrews. The sketch of the terrain of that hole made by Dr. MacKenzie, the eminent golf course architect, is the best one available and I have used it here to indicate the interesting problems presented by the ground and the four different ways in which it is tackled by players of varying degrees of power and skill. I saw Bobby Jones play it in still a fifth way. His tee shot was a long one straight down the Elysian Fields and his second hole high to the right of the green, from which position he easily obtained his four. In his foursome match playing with Watts Gunn, he sliced his tee shot into an awkward position near the boundary on the right. Watts Gunn, upon advice from his caddie and after consultation with Bobby, played his second shot from some rather tenacious rough well out to the left on the line taken by C. No one that I saw during the Cup matches attempted to take the line chosen by B., which is, as the reader will see, the direct line but one extremely dangerous to travel.

The next hole I should choose is the eighth at St. Andrews and it is one which I think few of our players will remember with pleasure. They all played high in the air, directly over the small pot at the green's edge. None of their shots, so far as I saw, stayed anywhere near the hole. The eighth measures 140 yards

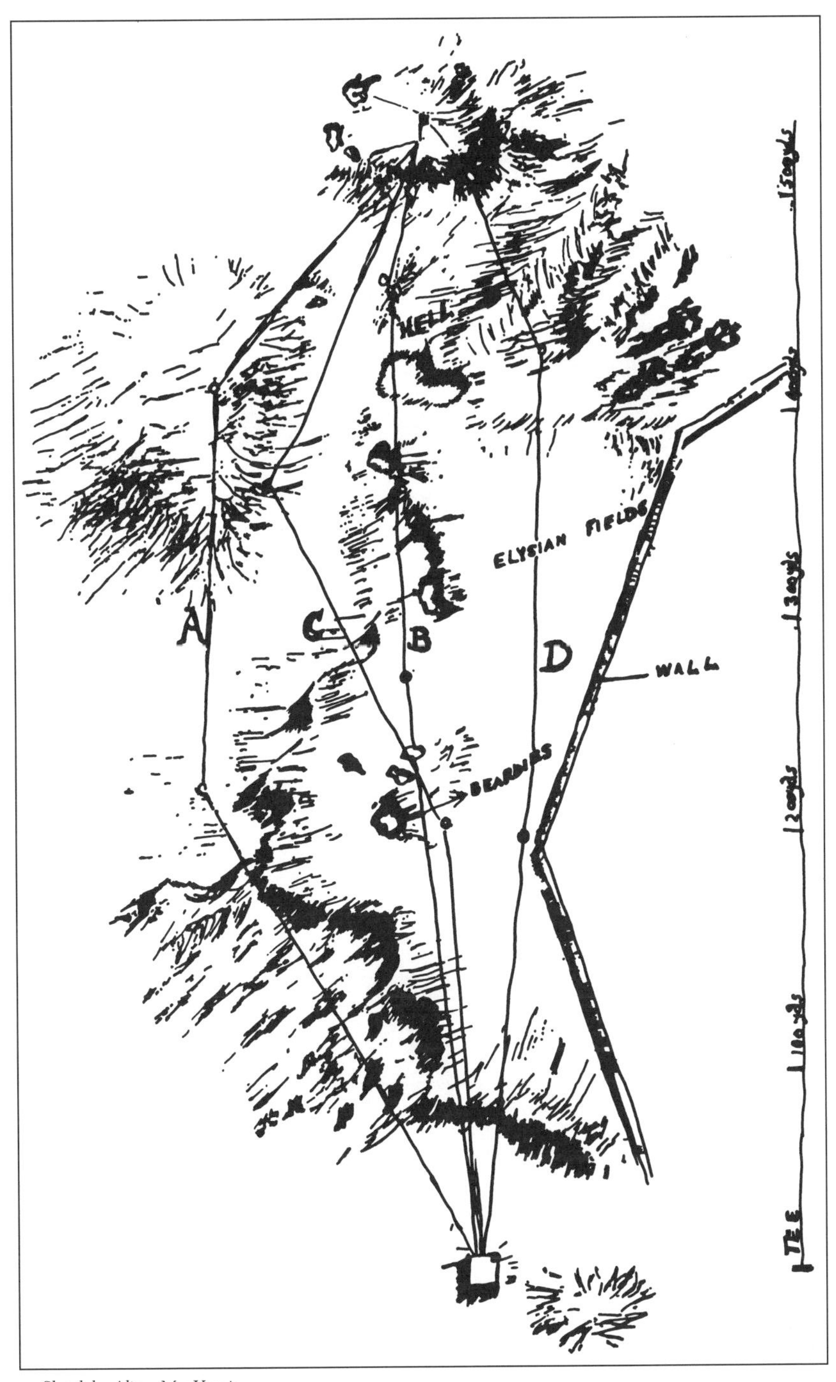

Sketch by Alister MacKenzie

THIS DIAGRAM OF THE FOURTEENTH HOLE AT ST. ANDREWS SHOWS THE FOUR DIFFERENT ROUTES FROM TEE TO GREEN WHICH MAY BE CHOSEN IN PLAYING THE FAMOUS THREE-SHOT HOLE, DEPENDING ON THE STRATEGY ADOPTED IN THE PLAY.

and the green is quite large. About 100 yards from the tee is an offensive looking ridge which is the making of this hole. It runs at an angle from a hollow of rough grass and bends to a deep pot bunker guarding the left of the green. The ideal ball would seem to be a high one with a touch of slice. This would carry the pot, but the green is hard and fast, and one wonders if he can put enough bite on the ball to stop near the cup.

A ball with a slight pull over the ridge has at least twenty yards more leeway and, if the wind be not too strong, may be the better shot. The most dangerous but most effective shot would be a pitch and run. This should, if perfectly played, strike at the base of the ridge, bound over it and run close to the hole. What fascinating problems are presented here!

I saw a great shot played at this hole by Roger Wethered in a practice round. I was standing near Edward Blackwell talking to a compatriot of mine when a low running ball hit the ridge. It veered abruptly to the left and, just escaping the pot, lay dead to the hole.

My companion exclaimed, "What a rotten lucky shot!" I remarked that probably Wethered had purposely played it that way. My friend hooted the suggestion and we referred to Mr. Blackwell to decide the question. "It was a remarkably fine shot and the exact one to play," he informed us.

The eleventh at St. Andrews is to my mind the best of all one shot holes. Similar holes have been built at the National, Garden City and Sunningdale, not to speak of the many others. "The green here is somewhat smaller," I am quoting from *The Links*, "and the distance somewhat longer than at the eighth. The Cockle, or Shelly, bunker runs in from the right, about 110 yards from the tee. At the left of the green lies Hill Bunker and just beyond the green "the sandy horrors of Eden," while at the right is a small pot.

Within the area of the green, on a line to its center, yawns Strath—a terrifying cavity from two to eight feet deep. Looking at this nest of hazards, one could sympathize with a champion, facing this hole in a critical round, if he were heard to pray: 'O Lord, be merciful.' Yet this hole may well be played, and often is well played by the local talent, with a putter."

There are other fine holes on the Old Course although these are perhaps the most interesting if we except the seventeenth, thought by many to be the best of them all.

The one mentioned and diagrammed indicates what can be done by golf course architects to make holes testing to the champion and yet enjoyable to those of lesser skill. It is obvious that one cannot make a course interesting or worthwhile without penalties. But these should not be placed with the idea of invariably catching the wayward, but rather with the thought of protecting the desirable line of play from an assault awkward and inept.

Let the old boy roll his ball along the ground, but insist that he keep in the groove. Let the youth slice and hook, but teach him that not even champions can play the hole from where he lies.

Let the boy pitch who will learn no other shot. He will discover in time that one or two of the holes cannot be mastered in that manner. Such is the cunning of St. Andrews and that is why it grows more and more entrancing as the years roll by.

There are three fine courses at St. Andrews: The Old Course, The New Course, and The Eden. The New Course is sometimes spoken of as the second best course in Scotland, while The Eden, designed by Harry Colt, would be considered a masterpiece in any other environment. But who plays either of these courses if he can find a starting time on the Old Course? Both new courses were the product of fine golfers and first rate architects, while the Old Course remains fatherless, like many a glorious cathedral. It is in fact the product of evolution. First there were but six holes and the play out and in was along the same bit of narrow fairway with whins, heather, and other horrors crowding in on both sides.

Even after the course was extended to its present length, there was but a single fairway out and in, although it was customary to change frequently the line of play. This week the players went out on the left and returned on the right, while the next week the line of play was reversed. Thus St. Andrews, which we so admire now, was in its earlier day one of the narrowest, most difficult, punishing and testing courses of that time or any other.

The need for space to supply the requirements of an increasing number of golfers, and the trampling and divots of many generations, have altered the Old Course and given us today what we may call the ideal course. Rubber has displaced Guttie which in its time took the place of the feather ball. Each change has made the game easier. Clubs of every conceivable design have displaced the spoons of earlier days and these new and clever instruments have made many of us golfers who would not otherwise play the game. The whins and heather have been beaten back; the greens and fairways have been greatly widened; the putting has been taken from the abrupt slopes and hollows and placed rather more on the level; and all this no doubt indicates degeneracy.

However, it suits us admirably and if Bobby Jones, now "cock o' the green," will only continue to speak well of our

Ralph W. Miller Golf Library

THE EIGHTEENTH GREEN AND ROYAL AND ANCIENT CLUBHOUSE AT THE OLD COURSE AT ST. ANDREWS.

ideal, why should we old boys, scuffling the ball along the ground, wince when we read in James Balfour or in Johnny Low of the terrors of the Old Course three quarters of a century ago when the great Allan Robertson ruled the roost?

~

Editor's Note
Dr. MacKenzie and Pleasurable Golf Courses

During the mid-1920s, English golf architect Alister MacKenzie responded to several articles in *Golf Illustrated* magazine by writing lengthy and sometimes spiteful replies. In one of his most spirited, MacKenzie defended the Portland Course at Troon after it came under attack from several 1923 British Open qualifying contestants, including Gene Sarazen. It was not the last time MacKenzie and Sarazen would wrangle, but it was their most visible public debate. A few years later in *Pacific Golf and Motor Magazine*, MacKenzie called Sarazen a "vandal" for suggesting that the cup be enlarged so as to de-emphasize putting.

In the following article, "Pleasurable Golf Courses," Dr. MacKenzie questions the work of golf writer Joshua Crane, who published an odd article in the January, 1926, *Golf Illustrated.* Crane suggested a codified method for rating famous golf courses which favored more difficult layouts over those with charm, character, and strategy.

However, "Pleasurable Golf Courses" is more than just MacKenzie venting his frustration at Crane. It is a wonderfully concise explanation of what makes St. Andrews special, the differences between the penal and strategic schools of architecture, and most of all, it provides a distinct description of the design elements which make golf pleasurable.

G.S.

~

Pleasurable Golf Courses
The Effort to Eliminate Luck Has Made Many Bad Courses

by Dr. Alister MacKenzie
Golf Illustrated
April 1926

A pleasurable golf course is not necessarily one that appeals at first sight, but rather one that grows on the player like good music, good painting, or good anything else. I also venture to suggest that a pleasurable course is synonymous with a good one. No course can give lasting pleasure unless it is a good test of golf. I also submit that no course can be really first rate unless it appeals to all classes of players.

We all play golf for the health and pleasurable excitement it gives us, and if a golf course fails to give pleasure to the largest number, it lacks something which prevents its being first class. Most of us can recall widely advertised courses in America and Britain which fail in this respect.

I have recently seen an article by Joshua Crane on the rating of famous golf courses. It is difficult to read his article without a feeling of intense irritation. His views show a similar mentality to that which in Britain gave us Tom Dunn's and other dreary courses thirty years ago, and which (thank goodness) have been in most cases completely reconstructed. He rates Muirfield as the best and poor old St. Andrews as the worst of our famous golf courses, whereas any architect in Britain or America who has achieved any marked success in creating popular courses will reverse his rating. In his article on the new course at Sunningdale, he rates it much higher than the old course at St. Andrews, whereas the writer who collaborated with Mr. Colt in designing it would never dream of putting it anywhere near the same class. The Old Course at St. Andrews rarely appeals at first sight, and it not infrequently takes years before scoffers succumb to its many virtues, but the fact remains that it is the only course which has remained unaltered for scores of years, and is as popular today as in the days of the "gutty" ball, and the writer ventures to prophesy that it will remain unaltered during the lifetime of all my readers. It is a course which caters to a higher standard of golf than any one has attained today, and yet it is extremely pleasurable to the old gentleman who cannot drive a ball any further than a lusty youth could kick one.

I know of one ex-amateur British champion who approaches and putts as well as he ever did, but yet cannot drive as far as the average penal hazard placed on many an indifferent inland course to catch a topped shot. Yet, at St. Andrews he is still a formidable opponent, as there is always some route open to a short and accurate player. Should an ex-amateur champion be deprived of the joy of playing golf in his old age? And yet many courses are now being made impossible for a player of his caliber. A first-class course like St. Andrews is pleasurable to all ages, all sexes, and players of all handicaps. At St. Andrews there are always routes open to players of different handicaps, and one might quote in particular the twelfth, thirteenth, fourteenth, fifteenth, sixteenth and seventeenth holes there. It is

The Spirit of St. Andrews *(Alister MacKenzie)*

AN ENTIRELY ARTIFICIAL HOLE—GIBRALTAR, EIGHTH HOLE, 160 YARDS, AT MOORTOWN GOLF COURSE, ENGLAND. CONSIDERED BY MANY THE BEST SHORT HOLE IN ENGLAND.

not difficult to create holes on any inland course of similar characters.

There are many bad golf courses made in an attempt to eliminate the element of luck—a mistake, surely. Luck is the zest of life, as well as of golf.

There are two schools of thought in golf; the penal school and the strategic school. The penal schools in their well intentioned effort to eliminate luck, simply succeed in accentuating it, and in constructing golf courses so dull and uninteresting and devoid of suspense and thrills that no one wishes to play them. The strategic school, on the other hand, are the small minority of golfers who subscribe to the doctrine of Mr. John L. Low "that no bunker is unfair, wherever it is placed"—and "that an error of judgment, to say the least of it, has always been perpetrated if a ball is trapped by a hazard." They consider that the indifferent player should be allowed enough rope to hang himself and that generally the punishment for a bad shot should not be an immediate one, but should be postponed so that the player is in a bad strategic position for attacking the green. In other words, there should be at least one, if not more, broad roads that lead to destruction and a narrow and hazardous road that leads to salvation.

What does it matter if the poor player can putt all the way from tee to green, provided that he has to zigzag so frequently that he takes six or seven putts to reach it?

The strategic school consists of the pioneers who have been responsible for the many excellent golf courses in Britain and America. In America, I believe, the true spirit of golf is rapidly becoming more prevalent than it is in Scotland, the home of golf. Americans are the most earnest seekers of the truth, and do not make the mistake so prevalent in England that because they are players bordering on scratch they have little to learn about golf courses.

During my visit to America I have been much impressed by the pains golf course architects have taken to read all the literature there is on the subject of golf course architecture. As an example, the president of an athletic club in California, consisting of over five thousand members, showed me a copy of a letter he had sent to England asking for one hundred copies of a book on golf course architecture so he could distribute these to the principal golf players in his club.

It is this spirit of desire to learn which is rapidly creating in America some of the best and most pleasurable golf courses in the world.

In conclusion, I may say that it is a great pity that a gifted and talented golfer like Joshua Crane has written these articles

Photo by Lynn Shackelford

THE "HIGH HOLE IN," THE PAR-3 ELEVENTH HOLE ON THE OLD COURSE AT ST. ANDREWS.

on the grading of golf courses. They have excited much attention in Britain, and are likely to give the impression that Americans lack the adventurous spirit of the true sportsman, whereas the contrary is the case, and I may say that in an extensive tour from East to West, I have not met an American golfer of any prominence who does not whole-heartedly condemn Mr. Crane's revolutionary views.

~

Editor's Note
O.B. Keeler and the Links

O.B. Keeler was present at most of the landmark occasions in the illustrious career of Bobby Jones, and it was Keeler who documented Jones' life and times to give us an unparalleled look at perhaps the greatest golfer of all time. In introducing Keeler's posthumously published articles, *The Bobby Jones Story*, Jones summed up their relationship:

> O.B. Keeler and I enjoyed a very real partnership for the better part of twenty years. We traveled thousands of miles together, we lived our golf tournaments together, we wrote a book, did a radio series, and two motion pictures series, all in the closest and most harmonious collaboration. I doubt if ever such a relationship existed between performer and reporter in sport or elsewhere.

As an *Atlanta Journal* writer for 50 years, Keeler followed Jones to all of his tournament stops including his 1926 voyage overseas to Scotland for the British Amateur, the Walker Cup, and the British Open. Jones reached the semifinals of the Amateur at Muirfield, then took both of his matches at St. Andrews in the Walker Cup for the victorious U.S. team. He completed his stay in the British Isles by winning the Open Championship at Lytham and St. Anne's. All the while, Keeler watched and observed the links where the competitions took place and upon returning to the United States, filed this outstanding description of overseas golf for *The American Golfer* magazine.

G.S.

~

What I Saw of British Links

by O.B. Keeler
The American Golfer
September 1926

I was glad of the opportunity on the recent golfing invasion of Great Britain to look at some of the famous golf courses and links and form some opinions of my own as to their merits when compared with our American championship and other courses and links, and before we get any farther let us lapse for a moment into the didactic and get this business of "course" and "links" straightened out. Over here, we are prone to employ these terms synonymously, partly from carelessness and partly because links is a brief word with an "I" in it and fits neatly into headlines. But while every links might be termed a golf course it would be highly improper, on the other side, to term most golf courses a links—links, by the way, being singular in significance though plural enough in form. A links is a seaside golf course, and an inland golf course is not a links. George Greenwood explained the singularity of the word to me; I already was apprised of the difference between a links and a course. Mr. Greenwood omitted, or did not deem it necessary, to explain if links was to be used as a plural form as well as singular, of it the plural form would be linkses. I assume the former.

Anyway, I found the links and courses of Britain interesting and impressive, and in several outstanding cases of immense educational value. I did not play over any of them, studying them vicariously, you might say. In addition to being one of the sixteen American males of voting age who have never seen "Abie's Irish Rose," I now am the only American duffer who ever went to St. Andrews and did not play a round on the famous "Old Course." But I can tell ever so much more about a course, watching other people play it.

When playing it myself, I find my attention rather microscopically restricted to mere details, such as pot-bunkers, burns, and the like, many of them having no reasonable connection with the hole for which I am bound. I miss the sweep and scope of the general layout, if any, while pottering around behind gooseberry bushes and performing feeble excavatory ceremonials in ditches and traps . . . By the way, our British cousins regard our term "trap" as a colloquialism, as also "cup" for hole.

Most of all I had heard of St. Andrews, and not all of what I had heard was complimentary. Never mind what I fancied I was looking for, when I got there with the Walker Cup team. What I found was, to quote Bobby Jones, a classic golf course.

"But what is the difference between a good course over there and a good course over here?" I have been asked a hundred times.

In a word, the main difference is that a good course over there is a good deal harder to play. It is not longer, and usually not as hard. There are no more traps—pardon! bunkers—and usually not so many. The rough sometimes is rougher, as when it consists mainly of heather or gorse. The turf is fine and the greens, depending more on the weather than ours, not being artificially sprinkled, are extremely good, as we saw them on this tour, but more variable.

But where we in America, with true Yankee ingenuity, have gone in for what we assume to be scientific golf architecture,

The American Golfer

CHICK EVANS PLAYING FROM THE ROAD WHICH RUNS BACK OF THE GREEN ON THE SEVENTEENTH HOLE AT ST. ANDREWS. THIS HOLE HAS BEEN THE GRAVE OF MANY A PROMISING SCORE.

with three hundred bunkers to the course, and carefully trapped fairways, and small greens targeted among bunkers, and each shot carefully measured off and prescribed—where we fondly present to the world a scientific championship course (and I do not say it isn't, by any means), over there they have a notion of letting nature take its course.

Without mentioning any names, which might be held unjustifiably invidious, I recall at least three superb and real championship tests of golf in the United States, on which I have seen national events played, and in all the rounds I witnessed on them, not one of the three courses needed to be played differently on Tuesday from the way it was played Monday, or at a variance Wednesday afternoon from the correct mode on Wednesday morning.

The British mode of allowing nature to takes its course consists mainly in permitting the wind to blow where it listeth, which it assuredly is going to do—in Britain—anyway.

The wind makes a difference, and the difference is enormous. Why there should be so much more apparent wind about the British Isles than about even our pet seaside links I am not prepared to say. But there is. Inland as far as forty and fifty miles, at James Braid's course, Walton Heath, our brave lads were saluted with a gale the first time they went out to practice after landing, which extracted from Watts Gunn the sapient comment:

> "Gee—the course wouldn't be so hard if the wind didn't blow."

He had just finished a well-played 79. All our boys had a fine battle getting below 80.

That is the point. The wind always blows, at Walton Heath, and that is forty miles inland. Also, the rough is heather and gorse.

Now, I did not become a wholehearted admirer of all the British courses and links we saw. There is the Royal St. George's at Sandwich—my honest opinion of that famous links would be ill received by the members, who rather fancy the course was laid out by St. Andrew himself. It is indubitably interesting, even exciting. But the huge dunes and undulations and hills and hummocks that make up almost all the fairway and rough and some of the greens give too much play for the scampish finger of luck, even to suit one who fancies that Americans are trying too industriously to scientificalize the game. Jesse Guilford, who speaks infrequently but usually to the point, offered what I thought the best criticism of the Royal St. George topography:

> "When you're playing this links," said the Great Excavator, plodding along down a valley-fairway, "you can't see any of it but the hole you're playing, and darned little of that!"

Too many blind shots; too many eccentric lies—and always a rollicking gale—conspire to make Sandwich a somewhat dizzy test for the stranger. And yet it can be shot in low figures. Was it not on the first nine at Sandwich that Chick Evans in the British Amateur championship of 1914 went to the turn in par, and was 5 down to Charlie Macfarlane, who had done a neat 31 with a 6 on a par 4 hole?

Rye we found also undulating, and windy, and I regarded it as a better course than Sandwich, and liked neither of them by any means so much as Sunningdale, an inland course with heather about. But then I was prejudiced in favor of Sunningdale, after Bobby did that 66 and that 68 on it. So was Bobby. He said he would like to take that golf course home with him. Yet it is no part of a set-up. Prior to the qualifying rounds there this summer the course record was 70, and 69 was the best anyone did, except Bobby.

The small employment of pitching tools is a leading characteristic of Sunningdale. In 36 holes Bobby used his mashie twice and his mashie-niblick once. Most of his shots to the green were full iron bangs—with an occasional brassie. And anybody knows it is the drive-and-pitch courses where most of the hot scoring is done.

Now St. Andrews, which I have heard a bit slanged at home and also abroad, the burden of the complaint being that it is unlike any other golf course—which so far as I know is meticulously true.

The grand old course needs no feeble defense from me. But with further regard for the American taste and tendency in championship tests, permit me to quote Bobby Jones, who did a good deal of golf studying on that trip. He is speaking of St. Andrews, the Old Course, where the International Match was playing:

> "Employing a comparison with our own best courses in America," said he, "I have found that most of our courses, especially those inland, may be played correctly the same way round after round. The holes really are laid out scientifically; visibility is stressed; you can see what you have to do virtually all the time; and when once you learn how to do it, you can go right ahead, next day, and the next day, and the day after that.
>
> "Not at St. Andrews. The course is broad and open, and the rough is distant, and the fairways confront you in almost every direction. The greens are huge. And with all that, and with almost all the visible universe to shoot into, you may plume yourself on any round of 72 to 75 that falls to your fortune there. From tee after tee, you are offered about all the real estate you can cover, for your drive. But you would better place that drive with some thought and exactness, or your second shot will be a terror. The fourteenth hole, for example—I think it perhaps the finest on the course—may be played four different ways, all correct and widely at variance, according to the wind. And the wind is a worthy foe. It is just as likely to oppose you all the way out, and turn as you turn, and battle you all the way back. Or it may follow you around

> the entire horseshoe. You must use something beside shots and clubs, playing St. Andrews. I can learn more golf in a week on that course than in a year on many a sterling championship test in America."

There are only two short holes on St. Andrews, the length is 6,572 yards, and par is a hard 73. At some holes, under varying wind conditions, it becomes expedient to play your second shot toward the green from widely different positions. In their match against Tolley and Jamieson in the foursomes, Bobby asked Watts to drive from one tee far off line—not at all toward the green. Watts obediently played the shot as requested, and Bobby had a grand opening to bang the ball with a full pitch straight into the wind's eye—the very easiest kind of an approach shot to control, especially where the greens either are flat or slope slightly away from you, as at St. Andrews. Played in the obvious direction, the drive would have left him an almost impossible approach in a sweeping cross-wind. There is nothing obvious about St. Andrews.

Come to think of it, I am beginning to think that the idea of flat greens or slightly falling greens is more truly scientific than the American plan of small greens targeted or banked to stop almost any shot that hits them. Only a real golf shot will hold those big, flat, or slightly retreating greens; and you may have to exercise yourself between the ears in selecting the shot to play.

~

. . . although golf architecture may be a curious and irregular form of architecture, it is architecture none the less. It has to do with building, planning and constructing in as true a sense as the most ambitious works of genius with which the art is usually associated. Cathedrals, bungalows, gardens and golf courses may appear to be conflicting examples of constructive ability, yet the principles governing them follow precisely on the same lines. They all involve the same processes, however much the processes may appear to differ.

—H.N. Wethered and Tom Simpson

~

Part II

Architecture

Golf architecture has been defined in many ways and the next four essays manage to outline the key elements in constructing and building a course, though each uses a different means to prove its point. C.B. Macdonald approaches golf architecture in a rather forthright manner. He also manages, perhaps better than anyone, to convey why architecture should be taken seriously if we are to enjoy our courses. Macdonald's "Architecture" chapter, extracted from his book *Scotland's Gift—Golf*, is one of the finest essays ever written on design. Shinnecock Hills architect William Flynn brings a more diplomatic approach to design, detailing the building blocks for getting your project off the ground. However, Flynn also goes beyond the basics and makes several definitive statements on architecture in "The First Step" and its sequel, "Analysis of Layout." A.W. Tillinghast ends Part II by explaining what makes natural sites so important in "The Ideal Course—Rugged and Natural."

~

Editor's Note
C.B. Macdonald and Architecture

Charles Blair Macdonald left Chicago at the age of sixteen for two years of study at the University of St. Andrews. When he departed in 1876, young C.B. had never heard of golf, but the wonderful town and the "home of golf" soon changed his mind. His grandfather, a member of the Royal and Ancient Golf Club and a St. Andrews resident, took Charles to Old Tom Morris' Golf Shop to purchase a few clubs, and immediately Macdonald's sixty-year love affair with golf began.

Over the next two years, Macdonald's affection for St. Andrews flourished and his relationship with the Morrises—Old Tom, Young Tom, and Jamie—fashioned him into an credible player, able to hold his end up in matches. He became especially close with Young Tom and played most of his golf with the Morrises. During these matches, Macdonald absorbed the strategy and subtlety of the Old Course and several of the other nearby links.

After his two-year study abroad, C.B. Macdonald returned in 1878 to an America that had little interest in golf. In 1892, with the sport finally catching on in the States, he built the first nine holes of the original Chicago Golf Club. Macdonald later persuaded the club to buy a more suitable piece of property in Wheaton, Illinois, where he would construct the first formal 18-hole course in the United States. Macdonald's longtime construction and engineering associate, Seth Raynor, later made significant changes to the design in 1923, but Chicago Golf Club remains perhaps America's least known architectural masterpiece.

The nation's premier amateur golfer for a time, Macdonald's influence and persistence led to the 1895 creation of the United States Golf Association. He spent most of the next ten years fostering the USGA and playing competitive golf before turning his focus toward creating one of the most charismatic and brilliant golf courses any man has ever built. The opening of The National Golf Links in 1911 marked the beginning of the twenty-five year "Golden Age" of American golf architecture, the most productive period in our nation's history for distinguished golf course designs.

To build The National Golf Links, Macdonald formed a syndicate and purchased a rolling piece of land on Long Island in 1906, setting out to design a course that would embody the best elements of the great links of Scotland and England. It included holes built on the principle of Macdonald's favorites from North Berwick, St. Andrews, Prestwick, and Royal St. George's, and incorporated many other architectural elements that Macdonald learned from Old Tom Morris and the Scottish links. Macdonald also introduced several original strategic and aesthetic elements at The National, including enormous greens, vast areas of sand, and water hazards.

The National Golf Links quickly became America's version of the Old Course at St. Andrews. It was, and still is, a national treasure that every golf architect should visit before practicing design. Macdonald himself obsessed over every detail at the National, nurturing it for nearly twenty years.

Macdonald also created several other outstanding courses, each built and co-designed under the devoted supervision of Seth Raynor: Yale University's course in Connecticut; The Creek, Piping Rock, and Fishers Island in New York; St. Louis Country Club; and Mid-Ocean in Bermuda. Macdonald and Raynor also built two revered and now defunct courses on Long Island, Lido Golf Club and The Links.

In the following essay we find perhaps the most concise and genuine thesis ever written on design. Macdonald covers many topics in a remarkably small space and manages to make you laugh as you read his candid and sometimes tyrannical thoughts.

The prolific English golf writer Alistair Cooke best described the historical significance of Macdonald's book, and in particular, his architecture essay when he wrote: "What makes it a necessity is Macdonald's remarkable instinct (by no means shared even by some of the greatest golfers) for the principles of golf architecture. Here, too, he was not an apprentice to a well-established profession. He was more like a young Aristotle, inventing the specialty as he went, deducing first principles ("a play has a beginning, a middle, and an end") which nobody before had thought of."

G.S.

~

Architecture

by Charles Blair Macdonald
1928

To the solid ground of Nature trusts the mind that builds for aye.
—Coleridge

To my mind every aspirant who wishes to excel in golf architecture should learn by heart and endeavor to absorb the spirit of the following lines, copied from "The Art of Landscape Architecture," written by the great Humphrey Repton in 1797:

> If it should appear that, instead of displaying new doctrines or furnishing novel ideas, this volume serves rather by a new method to elucidate old established principles, and to confirm long received opinions, I can only plead in my excuse that true taste, in every art, consists more in adapting tried expedients to peculiar circumstances than in that inordinate thirst after novelty, the characteristic of uncultivated minds, which from the facility of inventing wild theories, without experience, are apt to suppose that taste is displayed by novelty, genius by innovation, and that every change must necessarily tend to improvement.

Viewing the monstrosities created on many modern golf courses which are a travesty on Nature, no golfer can but shudder for the soul of golf. It would seem that in this striving after "novelty and innovation," many builders of golf courses believe they are elevating the game. But what a sad contemplation!

Motoring to Southampton, I pass a goodly number of new courses. As I view the putting-greens it appears to me they are all built similarly, more or less of a bowl or saucer type, then built up toward the back of the green, and then scalloped with an irregular line of low, waving mounds or hillocks, the putting-green for all the world resembling a pie-faced woman with a marcel wave. I do not believe any one ever saw in nature anything approaching these home-made putting-greens. Then scattered over the side of the fairway are mounds modeled after haycocks or chocolate-drops. The very soul of golf shrieks!

It is true that a group of golfers cannot always find an ideal terrain where they can build a fine golf course, but let the property be ever so flat, one may construct an interesting course.

The right length of holes can always be adopted; after that the character of the course depends upon the building of the putting-greens. Putting-greens to a golf course are what the face is to a portrait. The clothes the subject wears, the background, whether scenery or whether draperies—are simply accessories; the face tells the story and determines the character and quality—whether it is good or bad. So it is in golf; you can always build a putting-green. Teeing grounds, hazards, the fairway, rough, etc., are accessories.

T. Suffern Tailer's nine-hole golf course at Newport was built upon flat pasture land, but by building up the greens and bunkering them after classical models the course is a most interesting one, as evidenced by the great interest best golfers take in Tommy Tailer's annual Gold Mashie Tournament.

I shall not attempt to write a treatise on building golf courses under all conditions of climate, character of soil, character of undulations, and all that is incident to varying situations; I only have space to suggest that which one should strive to attain on whatever land may be given. Any kind of golf is better than no golf at all, so we must strive to get the best possible.

To my mind there is much nonsense preached regarding golf courses. It is not in my province to lay down to law—what is right or wrong—but so long as I am writing this story I am going to tell you what I think is best, regardless of any criticism there may be of it. Criticizing a golf course is like going into a man's family. The fond mother trots up her children for admiration. Only a boor would express anything else than a high opinion. So it is a thankless task to criticize a friend's home golf course. "Where ignorance is bliss tis folly to be wise." It is natural one should love his home course. He knows it, and with golf holes familiarity does not breed contempt, but quite the reverse.

This is best exemplified by experiences I have had in improving various holes on golf courses that I have fathered. Usually there is much objection to any alteration by the rank and file, but once done, when the club members become accustomed to the hole, they admit the justification for the alteration, which reminds one of Pope's lines:

> "Vice is a monster of so frightful mien
> As, to be hated, needs but to be seen;
> Yet seen too oft, familiar with her face,
> We first endure, then pity, then embrace."

I do not believe any one is qualified to pass on the merits of any one hole, let alone eighteen holes, unless he has played them under all the varying conditions possible—varying winds, rain, heat, frost, etc.

Wind I consider the finest asset in golf; in itself it is one of the greatest and most delightful accompaniments in the game. Without wind your course is always the same, but as the wind varies in velocity and from the various points of the compass, you not only have one course but you have many courses. Experts at the game temper their shots to the wind and learn how to make the most of it, pulling or slicing at will into the wind or hitting a low ball into the face of the wind. It is here that the true golfer excels. Low says: "A good player always prays for a windy day, but he must not pray too earnestly."

In designing a course try to lay out your holes so that they vary in direction. In this way a player gets an opportunity to play all the varying wind shots in a round. The National is noted for this. There is no wind from any point of the compass which favors a player for more than four or five holes.

A golf hole, humanly speaking, is like life, in as much as one cannot judge justly of any person's character the first time one meets him. Sometimes it takes years to discover and appreciate hidden qualities which only time discloses, and he usually discloses them on the links. No real lover of golf with artistic understanding would undertake to measure the quality or fascination of a golf hole by yard-stick, any more than a critic of poetry would attempt to measure the supreme sentiment expressed in a poem by the same method. One can understand the meter, but one cannot measure the soul expressed. It is absolutely inconceivable.

I read much about ideal and classical courses; I used both these terms when I dreamed of the National, but I should like to make this distinction—no course can be ideal which is laid

Ralph W. Miller Golf Library

CHARLES BLAIR MACDONALD (FAR RIGHT) AND HIS SILENT GUESTS.

out through trees. Trees foreshorten the perspective and the wind has not full play. To get the full exaltation playing the game of golf one should, when passing from green to green as he gazes over the horizon, have a limitable sense of eternity, suggesting contemplation and imagination. This does not mean that a classical course cannot be laid out where trees are or where there is not the Atlantic, the Pacific or the North Sea to contemplate; but there is a vast difference between the ideal and a classical course. Yale is classical; St. Andrews, the National Golf Links and the Lido, the Mid-Ocean are ideal.

In speaking of trees, when I was in that lovely valley, White

Sulphur, where they have two exceedingly fine golf courses, the leaves fall like snowflakes over the greens. Thornton Lewis told me it cost them $500 a year to clear the putting greens of leaves in the fall. The price of clearing the greens of leaves, of course, doesn't change the character of the hole except that it requires an effort to pick them up or brush them aside in the line of one's putt or through the green when they are within one club-length of your ball. Many times your ball is hidden under a leaf, causing a search for it and delaying the game.

There are many moot questions argued by noted designers of golf courses. The character and placing of hazards has always been a bone of contention. Why, I cannot quite understand, because one has only to study the great holes which the world concedes are unexcelled. There should be every variety of hazard. Variety is not only "the spice of life" but it is the very foundation of golfing architecture. Diversity in nature is universal. Let your golfing architecture mirror it. An ideal or classical golf course demands variety, personality, and, above all, the charm of romance.

The undulations and the run of the ball tell the story as to how the hazards should be placed. Don't place them without experience. Generally speaking, as stated above, they should be of great variety, the greater the better, but always fair. By fair I mean where a player can extract the ball in one shot if reasonably well played in some direction.

Errors in play should be severely punished in finding hazards, but now the golfer wants his bunkers raked and all the unevenness of fairway rolled out. A player does not get the variety of stances or lies that in olden times one was sure to have. A hanging lie or a ball lying in any position other than level is a blemish to the modern golfer. The science and beauty of the

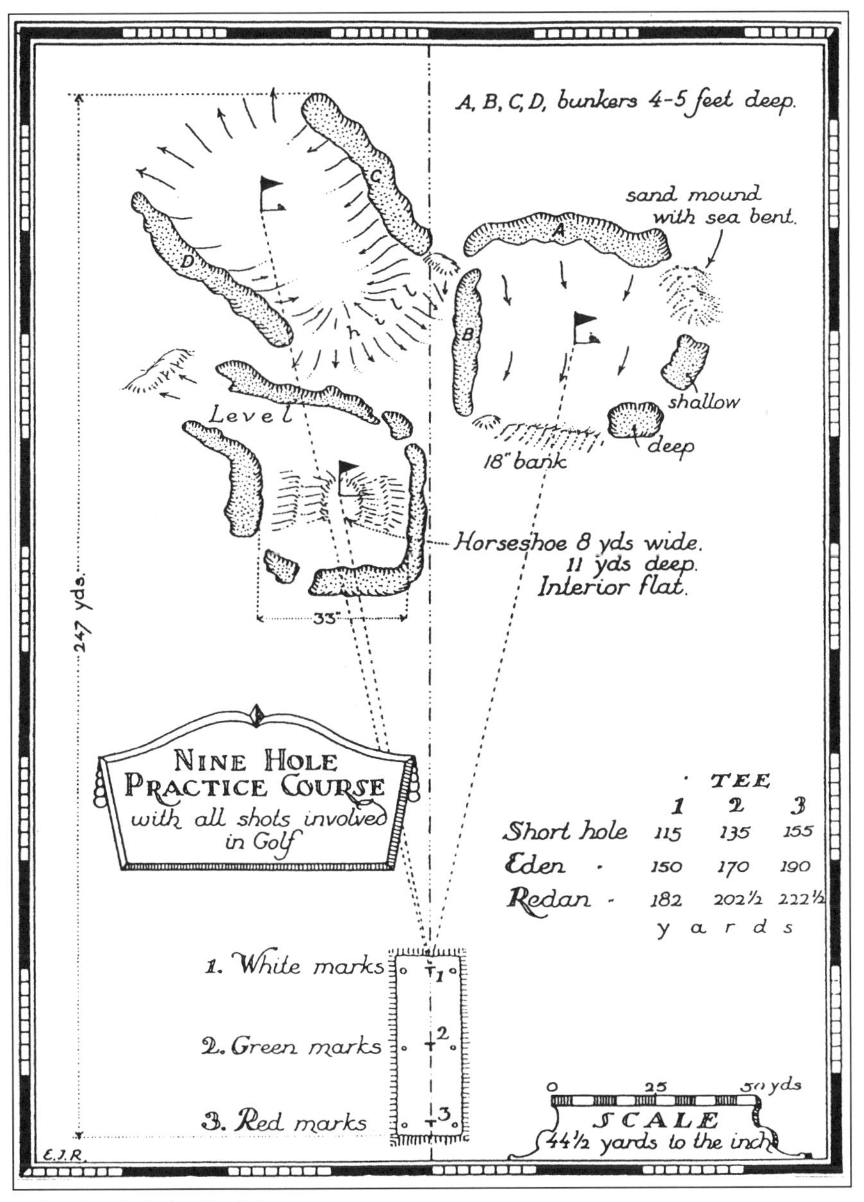

Sketch from Scotland's Gift—Golf

NINE HOLE PRACTICE COURSE

game is brought out by men having to play the ball from any stance. To play the game over a flat surface without undulations leaves nothing to the ingenuity of the player, and nothing is presented but an obvious and stereotyped series of hits. Today there seems to be a constant endeavor to make golf commonplace, to emasculate it, as it were, of its finer qualities.

Sand mounds are excellent grouped not where one has to climb up ten or fifteen feet, but say three to six feet, planted with sea bent so that the mounds will not blow away, but hold the sand in strong winds. The bent prevents lies where an expert player can take an iron club and easily make 100 to 140 yards recovery. Sand mounds can be created to conform truly with nature, but pot bunkers rarely do it on flat ground; never if they are not on the side of a mound or hill can they be made to look natural, and when building a course this should be borne in mind.

I do not believe in deep-ditch hazards; they always have long grass, usually very long in the bottom, are generally muddy and frequently have casual water, involving rules not generally understood. Water hazards should always be well defined. An arm of the sea can be wonderfully utilized, as can also a brook or stream; the former is much to be desired. I think Brancaster has one of the finest holes I know, where there are two arms of the sea running diagonally between the tee and the hole. Bushes never should be diagonally between the tee and the hole. Bushes never should be placed on the line of the hole, but can be so utilized on a dog-leg hole, where they are excellent, as they give severe punishment if they are not properly negotiated; also bushes say thirty yards from the middle of the course on the side, as rough similar to what St. Andrews used to be when it was at its best with the whins of some fifty years ago. Bushes, if placed too close, entail searching for one's ball, which is often lost. In such instances they should be thinned out. Searching for a lost ball is not a pleasant vocation, but since golf was first played a lost ball has always been a part of the game. So reconcile yourself to tradition.

Paths or roads should never be built introducing them as part of the course. If established before the course is laid out, leave them as natural hazards, but see that they are fair in their position.

I think there should be two holes which have fine large cross-bunkers protecting the green, both long two-shot holes; one, a hole resembling the Alps at Prestwick 410 to 430 yards in length; the other placed in a punch-bowl, say from 420 to 440 yards long. The cross-bunker in the latter case should be severe and very difficult, placed quite close to the green, for the reason that if one carries over the bunker he is home and protected on all sides. Holes of this character are of the very finest. Only the good golfers can reach these greens in two strokes; the others must play short so that the cross-bunker is no punishment to them unless they top their third shot. Ninety percent of the players cannot reach a 420-yard hole in two strokes, while the scratch men have to make really fine seconds, and if the wind is against them the second will be a very difficult second. Fine drives and fine long second shots give the finest emotion or thrill in golf. That is why two-shot holes are the best in golf.

I do not like cross-bunkers directly across the entire fairway to be carried from the tee unless built so that a player has his choice to "bite off as much as he can chew" by making them diagonal. A few such bunkers are excellent, diagonal or en echelon. Why a player should condemn the placing of any bunker I fail to comprehend. Any bunker properly placed is excellent.

Photo by Lynn Shackelford

WINDMILL AT THE NATIONAL GOLF LINKS

Johnny Low has stated that there is hardly such a thing as an unfair bunker. He is right. Variety is what one wants in a hole properly laid out. Long carries should not be compulsory, but if taken, the player should have a distinct advantage. Where there are bunkers at varying distances from the tee, the player has the option of going around or over according to his judgment. Bear in mind that a course must be absorbing and interesting, and not built for crack players only. Don't sacrifice accuracy for length.

A golf architect should endeavor never to construct what is known as a "trick green"; otherwise he will be suspected of being a card sharp. Don't seek an original idea in building a golf course. John LaFarge somewhere has said if "an idea were an original one it is safe to say it would not be a good one."

I should like also to suggest that the construction of bunkers on various courses should have an individuality entirely of their own which should arouse the love or hatred of intelligent golfers. Rest assured such holes are far too complex for one's absolute condemnation or absolute approval. Bunkers of this character are much to be desired on any golf course.

Golf architects should make use of ground sloping in toward the bunkers as a means of enlarging the scope and peril of the bunkers. An appreciation of this is very valuable in constructing bunkers.

Always bear in mind that golf courses are not laid out for scoring competitions, and as long as a good player can get out in one stroke, either forward, backward, or to one side, that bunker is not unfair. The risk of going into a bunker is self-imposed, so there is no reason why a player should condemn a bunker as unfair. If there were not more or less luck in a game it would not be worthy of the name, and a risk should be taken commensurate with the gravity of the situation which brings out the ideal factor, luck, and raises it above a mere record-breaking competition.

The principle of a dog-leg hole can be made a feature of several holes advantageously, usually from the tee, but there is no reason why one hole should not be featured by a dog-leg for the second shot.

In laying out the National here is a bit of advice I received from Charles F. Whigham, a very fine golf player:

"I. Don't be in a hurry to make many bunkers through the green until the course has been played on for a bit. Until you have played on a course a good deal in all winds and at all seasons, both wet and dry, it is impossible to gauge the length that good shots will get. This does not apply to bunkers round the greens. You can't have too many of these, as, granted that you have a fair sized good green, a good player ought to be able to put his ball upon it no matter how many bunkers there are round about.

"II. Don't make great big bunkers, but groups of small deep bunkers after St. Andrews' style. A big bunker is the flukiest thing I know. If you lie clean you are not punished at all, while if you lie in a bad hole, the strongest man can't hit the ball hard enough to get out."

Where I have large bunkers at the National, such as at the second hole, I plant sea bent. This prevents the sand from blowing and prevents the player from getting a full shot from the hazard.

I should always advise a place for three tees; one the championship tee, which would probably give pleasure to less than 5 percent of your club membership; then the regular tees, which two-thirds of your club membership really care to play, leaving about 30 percent of your club membership to play from the short tees, which means men who can drive only about 120 or 130 yards. This gives all your members a fair game and you do not take the joy out of their life.

I have not touched upon one fundamental in golf course construction, and that is, the necessity of having an abundant supply of water with good pressure to sprinkle the fairway from 150 to 270 yards from the tee and also the putting greens and the approach thereto. If the various courses in this country would water their fairway as above, you would hear very much less about 250 to 280-yard drives. Secondly, do not fail to have the low spots well drained.

In expressing my opinion on architecture in this chapter the reader must bear in mind I am assuming the golf course is being constructed on a desirable terrain. I have known a number of men of means with large estates who desired private eighteen-hole golf courses. I have always endeavored to deter them from building a private course of that character for the reason that they are very rarely kept up and it is difficult to get people to come and play. On a private course it is seldom that there are more than three or four playing, so it is more or less lonely.

I tried to deter Otto Kahn from building eighteen holes, but he thought he would like to have a fine lawn in front of his beautiful Long Island house. Of course, that in itself is worth while.

When Payne Whitney proposed building an eighteen-hole golf course on his property at Manhasset there was plenty of room, but the land was not adapted to it, and I persuaded him to build a nine-hole course and to build it on some twenty acres immediately back of his home. I grouped three classic holes in the center of the land which had to be played to at different angles. In this way it is perfectly simple to get nine good holes on a small acreage. It could easily take care of ten or twelve men playing, and I doubt very much if there were ever more than that number golfing over his course. It was beautifully kept up and one had as many fine golfing shots as he could have had on any golf course. This suggested to me the building of a practice ground on six acres by grouping three well-known classical greens, namely a short hole, an Eden hole, and a Redan. By making a tee play forty-two yards long by fifteen yards in width one could go to the front tee and play a ball to each green, then go to the middle tee and play a ball to each green, and then go to the third tee and play a ball to each green—that is, nine balls in all—then walk to the different greens and play them out. Having done this, take the balls back to the tee again instead of teeing them, drop them so you will get the fairway practice the same as if you were playing through the green.

I am appealing herewith a sketch of this situation. Any one in the vicinity of New York can, I am sure, at any time run down to Eddie Moore's place at Roslyn and see holes patterned more or less on this idea which I laid out a year or two ago.

I read a golf article not long since in which the writer called a "fetish" the copying of holes from the classical courses of

Photo by Lynn Shackelford

THE CLUBHOUSE AT THE NATIONAL GOLF LINKS

Great Britain, holes which have the testimony of all great golfers for more than a century or two past as being expressive of the best and noblest phases of the game.

Architecture is one of the five fine arts. If the critic's contention is true, then architecture must be a "fetish," as the basis of it is the copying of Greek and Roman architecture, Romanesque and Gothic, and in our own times among other forms, Georgian and Colonial architecture. One must have the gift of imagination to successfully apply the original to new situations. Surely there is nothing "fetish" about this.

I believe in reverencing anything in the life of man which has the testimony of the ages as being unexcelled, whether it be literature, paintings, poetry, tombs—even a golf hole.

Perhaps it may be apropos to close this chapter by quoting another great landscape architect, Prince Puckler:

> "Time is not able to bring forth new truths but only an unfolding of timeless truths."

~

Editor's Note
William Flynn and His Design Guidelines

In stark contrast to C.B. Macdonald's tirade on architecture, William Flynn's reflections on golf course design are a bit more subtle. But beware, Flynn was not afraid to speak his mind. In the following essays, "The First Step," and "Analysis of Layout" he touches on just about every major theme of course design and provides an excellent blueprint for approaching a new project.

A native of Massachusetts where he competed against 1913 U.S. Open winner Francis Ouimet as a youth, Flynn was a man of many diverse talents though it was golf course design that would eventually seize his attention. After designing Vermont's Hartwellville Country Club in 1911, Flynn moved to Philadelphia and worked on the construction crew of Merion Cricket Club's new course under the direction of Hugh Wilson.

Flynn and Wilson became friends and shared much of their knowledge during the early days of Merion. It was some 13 years later that Flynn would remodel the East Course under the ailing Wilson's direction. By the early '20s, Flynn was a full-time architect partnering with engineer Howard Toomey. Like another pair of Philadelphians, George Thomas and his construction supervisor Billy Bell, Flynn oversaw the artistic side of the design while Toomey supervised the engineering and construction details. Over the following ten years, the partnership of Toomey and Flynn would create some of America's finest strategic tests of golf, and yet to this day, they are perhaps the least recognized design team from the "Golden Age." Look at their well-known design work: Shinnecock Hills (complete revision of the course in 1931, creating the modern version), Cherry Hills in Colorado, and the Cascades course at The Homestead in Virginia.

Besides the redesign of Merion and some consulting at Pine Valley in conjunction with Thomas, it is Flynn and Toomey's lesser-known work that truly shines, including a group of brilliant Philadelphia area courses: Lancaster, Philadelphia Country Club, Philmont, Manufacturers, Huntington Valley, and Rolling Green. Additional Flynn and Toomey gems are The Country Club in Cleveland, Atlantic City Country Club, Indian Creek in Miami, and the Primrose Nine at The Country Club in Brookline, Massachusetts (part of which is used in their "composite course.")

What made Flynn's design work unique was a blend of strategic holes and a variety of styles, including vast wastes areas and bold sand-faced bunkering. Like his Philadelphia counterparts Thomas and Tillinghast, Flynn built a medley of holes long and short, and fashioned his routings around this premise of variety. And like so many of the architects of the 1920s and '30s, Flynn was able to clearly and succinctly describe his thoughts on architecture, as he demonstrates in the following essays.

G.S.

~

The First Step

by William Flynn
USGA Green Section Bulletin
June 1927

Much has been written about golf course architecture, about the theory of construction, as to why certain holes should be laid out in this way or that way, as to the cost of maintenance, and concerning the gradual improvement of the links. But it seems to me that too many of these authors fail to go back far enough. They ignore the basic fact that in order to have a satisfactory golf course you must first secure a suitable piece of land over which to lay it out.

And that first step is most important, for an unwise choice of terrain may prove so costly in the end as to almost, if not quite, bankrupt the whole project. So my advice to a club in process of organization, or to an old club that is forced by circumstances to seek other quarters, is to appoint a close-mouthed committee and have that committee scout around quietly so as to secure options on several available tracts of land without the secret leaking out that a golf club is in market for the property.

In the past it has been customary to purchase one or more old farms, with a stone house or two and an old barn, a creek or two, orchards and a few small hills and dales and then call in a Golf Architect and tell him to make the best of what the club owns.

The men on the purchasing committee, lacking special knowledge of engineering problems, frequently buy land because its scenic beauties appeal to them and without thought of the practical difficulties involved. So, when it comes to planning the course and the architect goes over the property he is forced to tell the committee that a really good layout is not possible unless expense is no object.

As the cost of construction is usually a very vital item in the budget the committee is much upset. And if it is decided to go ahead and build as good a course as the terrain and the club's treasury will permit the members never take as much pride in what they get as they would if there had been more latitude of choice.

If an option has been secured on three or four tracts of land the architect can go over each carefully and then tell the committee which he considers the best, and why, his reasons including its possibilities as the site for a really first-class course, for keeping down the cost of construction and for economical maintenance after it has been completed.

The golf architect who knows his business can tell the committee in plain, understandable English just why one tract should be chosen over the others. He can show by figures why the cost will be lower and the results more acceptable. He can explain why drainage and future upkeep must always be kept in mind, picture the grades that would have to be climbed on every round if this tract were chosen, or the chances of having fairways and greens flooded every year if another were selected.

There is no way of telling how much money has been literally tossed away by the lack of foresight in choosing land over which to build golf courses, but it must have been an enormous sum. Not only have mistakes been made in the past, but they are still being made by committees selecting the wrong properties for golf courses, and it does not seem fair to the host of golfers who annually pay the bills.

Any conscientious architect, by exercising tact and persuasion can save prospective clubs a great deal of unnecessary expense in making a proper selection of property for a new course, and this is all the more true when the architect is possessed of some knowledge of engineering.

In considering the man to select the property and lay out a golf course of the 1927 model a club should view the problem broadly. The committee in charge of the matter should inquire whether the man under consideration really cares for golf and its future, whether he cherishes the ideals of the game as handed down from the fathers and whether he has vision or whether he considers the building of courses as merely an easy way of making a good living.

They should visit some of his other efforts and find out if the members of clubs for whom he had built courses were satisfied. They should not engage him merely because he can prepare attractive plans. They should determine whether he has sufficient engineering ability to see to it that his plans are carried out as he intended and that all problems of future maintenance were provided for in advance.

The relative merits of the various architects available at the time the club wishes to secure its property and start work should be discussed with leading amateurs who have made a study of the theory of golf architecture and their opinions of the men under consideration secured. These amateur students would have little or no bias, for they greatly desire the betterment and advancement of the game.

Once the decision has been made and the architect named,

there should be a conference during which the committee should put all its cards on the table. It should be frank about what it wants, should tell the architect exactly how far the club can go financially and whether a really stiff course or one not quite so hard is desired.

The architect should look over the various tracts under option and eventually report to the committee which he considers the best for the particular purposes of the club in question and why he deems it so. When the choice has finally been made, the committee should outline any ideas or suggestions the various members may have in mind.

Some architects are faintly contemptuous of suggestions made by "amateurs," but the wise architect is aware that he does not know it all and that really good ideas are often developed in these conferences. He never turns down a sensible suggestion simply because it has been made by someone else. On the contrary he accepts it thankfully and promptly embodies it in his plans.

The committee has every right to disagree with its architect at that time, but not later when work has actually begun. During the preliminary proceedings it is up to the committee to advance every objection that comes to their minds, and it is up to the architect to prove to them that he is right when he is firmly convinced that such is the case.

He must explain to the committee clearly and convincingly just why one suggestion would not work, why another would be too costly, or why still another would draw the ironic laughter of the critics. Often objection is made that the course, as planned by the architect, would be "too hard," but these very objectors are usually the ones who boast about their "sporty course" after it has been completed.

The architect must be tactful, he must have his facts at his tongue's end and must be firm. But in the end, if he knows his job, he will get rid of unsound suggestions and obtain sanction for a course on which he is willing to stake his reputation. For no matter how many first-class links a man has built, just let him be overpersuaded by a committee to construct a freak course and the word at once goes around that he has lost his vision, is slipping fast down grade, and his reputation bursts like the proverbial bubble.

But after the architect's plans have been accepted and he has been told to go ahead the committee should, most distinctly, lay off. The architect should not be pestered with more suggestions as to changes, and so on, or bothered in any way by the individual members of the committee. He should be let alone to carry on the work after his own fashion.

It is impossible for most laymen to visualize what the completed course will look like during the early stages of construction. The whole terrain resembles a segment of land between the front-line trenches while the World War was on, and pessimistically minded members often want to fire the architect on the spot after just one brief glimpse of ploughed up fields, hundreds of tree stumps, deep ditches where water pipes are to go, and unsightly mounds and broad scars that eventually will be smooth greens and shining white sand traps.

If the club has sufficient confidence in the architect to hire his services it should be taken for granted that he is capable of laying out a course possessing both variety and interest, that it will be scientifically constructed and that once finished it can be maintained at reasonable expense.

No club should expect and no architect should consent to submit plans and specifications and then not supervise the construction. The architect's reputation depends on what he produces. If he allows others to carry out his ideas the chances are strongly in favor of confusion that will result in a botched job. In nine cases out of ten when a club attempts to construct the course, the man designated to superintend the job is not familiar with the architect's method, nor is he, perhaps, capable of interpreting the construction work being done as he conceived it.

It is often a very hard matter to convince a committee that their work has been done improperly because they are not familiar with seeing a course develop from the start and they always seem too easily satisfied with what has been done and are loathe to change it. The best results, I think, can be obtained when an architect has engineers associated with him who have been trained in his way of doing things and who are familiar with the problems connected with golf course construction, namely, soil structure, drainage, turf culture, and course maintenance.

With an organization of this kind nothing is left to guesswork or done in hit or miss fashion. Practically all of the construction problems have been worked out before a spade full of earth is moved. The advantages of having only one concern to deal with are obvious. Trained men will be in charge of all the various ramifications of the proposition and once finished, the engineering firm should stand back of its product. If anything is wrong, which is unlikely with an organization that knows its business, the firm will promptly put it right.

But, if a club has been dealing with many sub-contractors, it is hard to fix the responsibility and even more difficult to locate the man to blame and force him to make good. If a club, however, insists on attending to the actual construction of the course, the architect should insist on supervising the work. It is not fair to himself or to the club if his plans are not carried out as he envisioned them. No conscientious architect should accept more commissions during any season than he can give his personal attention to.

The plans first submitted by an architect should cover what might be well termed the framework of the course, but should be flexible in the matter of pits and bunkers. Those around the greens and certain traps just off the fairways may be fairly well determined in advance, but the location of the others can be determined better after the course has been completed and played on for a time.

In this connection it would be well for a club to retain its architect in an advisory capacity for a year or so after the actual work of construction has been finished. He will then be able to better determine the definite location of a complete bunkering system for the course and will be able to advise in the treatment of the course in preparing it for play. In this way the club can secure the best results and eventually find itself possessed of a course that will be satisfactory in every detail.

Analysis of Layout

by William S. Flynn
USGA Green Section Bulletin
October 1927

While there is no rule as to the number of the various types of holes to be incorporated in an eighteen-hole layout yet there are certain customs that most architects follow. In fact these customs have been handed down from the forefathers of golf and like many other things that have come down through the ages, they have their value.

The rule most generally adhered to is to have four holes of the course be one-shotters. To the majority of golfers the one-shot holes are the most interesting and there is no real reason why there should not be five one-shotters, particularly when such holes provide interest in the play and are of varying character.

On the other hand, a course with three outstanding one-shotters is much more desirable than one with four mediocre ones. It was also formerly thought that each course should have a three-shotter in each nine. Today, however, the thought prevails that one good three-shotter is sufficient unless some outstanding natural feature warrants putting in a second. Good three-shotters are the exception rather than the rule and unless the player has a specific thing to do on each shot other than slug, this type of hole becomes monotonous.

The principal consideration of the architect is to design his course in such a way as to hold the interest of the player from the first tee to the last green and to present the problems of the various holes in such a way that they register in the player's mind as he stands on the tee or on the fairway for the shot to the green.

The best way to whet the appetite and improve the game of any golfer is to offer an incentive and provide a reward for high class play, and by high class play is meant simply the best of which each individual is capable. Placing a premium on accuracy with due consideration for length should be the aim of all men who design golf courses, for accuracy in the play signifies skill and skill is generally the master of brute force.

It is impossible in considering types of holes for a course to suggest any positive sequence of alignment, for each layout should be designed to fit the particular ground on which it lies, although anything at all can be done with ground that is dead level and there are places in this broad land where clubs are compelled to use such terrain.

Flat ground has its disadvantages but it is the only ground that permits laying out holes where the sequence and lengths can be planned arbitrarily.

In discussing types of holes it is perhaps better to consider the question from the competitive or tournament play standpoint rather than from the everyday play, because in this connection only par golf is involved. In fitting the course to all classes in everyday play it is necessary to maintain relative values in the holes. This can only be done by using two and in some instances three tees to a hole, with the various players using the tee that fits their particular game.

The value of a hole is immediately lost when the 200-yard driver uses the back tee on a normal 420-yard hole. It is impossible for him to get home in two, whereas had the forward tee

USGA Green Section Bulletin *(Toomey and Flynn)*

ROLLING GREEN GOLF CLUB'S SIXTEENTH HOLE BY TOOMEY AND FLYNN.

40 to 50 yards ahead been used he would then have played a long iron or spoon shot to the green with a resultant thrill of satisfaction and at the same time be within his limitations.

A great many players are averse to using forward tees, perhaps because they were originally christened "ladies tees," but regardless of that fact it seems that a great deal more enjoyment could be had if golfers used the tee on the various holes that really suited their game. A little card tacked on their locker door with the following inscription might go a long way toward correcting their prejudice against the so-called "ladies tees":

GOLFERS, ATTENTION!

In order to accommodate all classes of players your club has gone to the expense of building forward, intermediate and back tees on many holes. These tees are kept in order and markers are placed on each one. Except in tournaments, please use the tee that fits your particular game and enjoy the course.

What holes should go to make up the average good course of today? The term average good course is used because it doesn't seem possible that any club will ever be in a position to build a course that might be considered ideal, a superb test of golf, because there are so many conflicting opinions in the average membership. The frame work of the course may be wonderful but its unfinished condition in regard to development of bunkering or scheme of play removes it a certain degree from the ideal.

With the exception of the short holes, assuming four to the layout, a golf course consists of 14 drives plus the par second and third shots, and the object should be to provide holes of proper length to accommodate the more important clubs after the drive has been made.

It naturally follows if this play is carried out that holes of character and variety can be had. The problems which should be developed on the various holes in the order of their importance are first—accuracy; second—carry; third—length, which includes carry and roll.

The premium on accuracy should carry the greatest reward, for this is the essence of any game. Carry, while slightly less valuable than accuracy, is important in that it promotes boldness. Length may be considered least important but this becomes quite a factor when a player is able to mold all three tests together.

In applying these problems or tests to the layout through the medium of bunkers, the architect has a great opportunity to display versatility. On one hole he may have a big diagonal bunker off the tee where the player takes as much risk as he feels capable of carrying and he is rewarded in his shot to the green commensurably with his first effort.

He may have a comparatively easy drive off another tee, and yet, if the ball strays slightly from the center of the fairway, his second shot to the green becomes increasingly hard.

By arranging the green bunkers in such a way as to invite play in from one side or the other he can also put a premium on placing the tee shot on the proper side of the fairway. When a test of length off the tee is presented, the best type is the cape or elbow where it takes a really big tee shot past a corner to permit reaching the green in par.

The problems may be diversified using one test off the tee on one hole, the same on the second shot of another hole; sometimes two or the same kind of the first and second shots of a hole; perhaps all tests, accuracy, carry, and length on another, but always juggling so as not to get sameness on succeeding holes.

While bunkers are thought by many to be put in as penalizers they are primarily installed to present a problem or a mode of play. If bunkers were used merely to punish bad shots there would have to be a complete revision of them on most courses.

The worst shots in golf are generally bad tops and wide hooks or slices and the player generally has sufficient penalty in these weaknesses, particularly when greens are properly protected.

America has developed a more or less stereotyped shot to the green that is the high, all-carry shot. This has been brought about no doubt by the fact that fairways and particularly approaches have gone unwatered during the summer when the ground has become hard. It is much simpler to play a high carry shot to a soft green which gets water than to attempt a pitch and run to a green with a cement-like approach.

In the first case, when all greens are watered a constant condition prevails, but in the case of the run-up approach the ball hits and is liable to bounce anywhere.

In order to cultivate the pitch and run, the run-up shot and the long-iron or wood with run, it is necessary to present a suitable playing condition on the approach and this can best be brought about by the architect insisting on a water system for fairways and by the greenkeeper making generous use of it.

Natural topographical features should always be developed in presenting problems in the play. As a matter of fact such features are much more to be desired than man-made tests for they are generally much more attractive.

USGA Green Section Bulletin *(Wilson and Flynn)*

THE PAR-3 SEVENTEENTH AT MERION. WILLIAM FLYNN OVERSAW MAJOR REVISIONS IN 1924 AT MERION FOR THE AILING HUGH WILSON. MR. FLYNN ALSO WORKED AT MERION FOR A SHORT TIME AS THEIR COURSE SUPERINTENDENT AND WORKED ON THE CONSTRUCTION CREW DURING THE ORIGINAL BUILDING OF MERION'S EAST COURSE.

One natural hazard, however, which is more or less of a nuisance is water. This is not nearly as bad when it parallels play and forms a picturesque landscape feature of the course. But when water is between the objective (the green or driving area) and the player, it may be that the man who plays only a foot short of the objective is much worse off than the one who makes a very poor shot that does not reach the water.

In the first place the player is penalized a stroke with no chance of recovering it whereas the second player having played a worse shot gets by without penalty and may regain lost ground with a fine second shot. Water hazards absolutely prohibit the recovery shot, perhaps the best shot in the game.

~

Editor's Note
Tillinghast and Natural Golf

A.W. Tillinghast, who later became one of America's most revered golf architects, did not start designing courses until he was in his early thirties. To that point, Tillie had been a well-established player, receiving his first golf lesson from Old Tom Morris during a stay at St. Andrews in the mid-1890s. His playing career included a 25th place finish in the 1910 U.S. Open, played at his home course, the Philadelphia Cricket Club. Tillie also played in the U.S. Amateur every year from 1905 to 1912 before turning pro in 1914. Like his friend, fellow Philadelphia Cricket Club member George C. Thomas Jr., Tillie grew up in a wealthy Philadelphia suburb and received his first design job through a family friend, Charles Worthington. Worthington reasoned that because of Tillinghast's playing ability, he could design a golf course—and he was right. Shawnee-on-the-Delaware, situated on the Delaware River in Pennsylvania, became a popular Poconos resort due in large part to the golf course. Soon after the opening of Shawnee, Tillie started his own design company and by the 1920s it was flourishing.

After completely redesigning and opening Baltusrol Golf Club in 1922, New York Athletic Club officials commissioned Tillinghast to give them 36-holes on wonderful terrain. The result: Winged Foot Golf Club, widely regarded as the best 36-hole facility in the United States. By 1930 his resume of classic courses was impressive: Ridgewood, Baltusrol and Somerset Hills in New Jersey; Winged Foot, Sleepy Hollow, Quaker Ridge in New York, and Brook Hollow in Texas; and redesigns of Newport in Rhode Island and Brooklawn in Connecticut. His final major design effort, the four municipal courses at New York Bethpage State Park, were built in 1936 and are considered by many to comprise the finest municipal golf complex in the United States. The Black Course at Bethpage will host the 2002 US Open.

Arguably, Tillie's most perfect design may be the San Francisco Golf Club, opened in 1915. It combines nearly every feature a golf course could possess: strategy, variety, diverse and rolling terrain, beauty, and superlative hazards. Though three holes were changed because of highway expansion, the club did a remarkable job disguising such a dramatic alteration.

During this productive career, Tillinghast served as editor of *Golf Illustrated* until 1934, writing numerous articles ranging from the basics of golf architecture to tournament updates and other important golf topics of the day. Tillinghast self-published two books of his fictional stories which were recently reprinted by the USGA. In the following article, one of Tillie's last for *Golf Illustrated*, he describes the ideal site for a golf course and his favorite natural feature: rugged dunes.

G.S.

~

The Ideal Course: Rugged and Natural

by A.W. Tillinghast
Golf Illustrated
February 1935

For a good many years back it has been my extremely pleasant business to select locations for golf courses, prepare plans and frequently to supervise their actual construction. Naturally my eye is peeled, as the saying goes, for impressively outstanding natural features. These are many but, of them all, I am sure that none moves me to greater enthusiasm than do sand dunes, big dunes contoured through the years by sweeping winds, and set off by wild grasses and drifted sands. And while we do succeed in approaching nature by artificial means, so frequently we are in utter despair in the realization of the utter futility of imitating the primitive contours and sweeps of the dunes. True enough, we have come rather close to it, but in my eyes there seems always to be lacking an indefinable something as the artificial work proclaims that it was made by man.

Consequently when we find the areas of sand dunes on or about the sites of proposed courses, it is peculiarly gratifying. And this is only too seldom in roaming over a continent as broad as ours, for the dunes bespeak the sea and the approaches to it as a general rule. There they belong, and it would be bad taste to attempt to reproduce them artificially along a sylvan fairway, far inland and away from their native heaths. However

Photo by Lynn Shackelford *(Old Tom Morris)*

THE SECOND HOLE AT ROYAL COUNTY DOWN, NORTHERN IRELAND—A MOST RUGGED AND NATURAL LANDSCAPE.

a thought of the rugged contours will relieve formality of lines when hazards are constructed anywhere.

No doubt my own appreciation of these rough fellows dates back into the latter part of the last century, some years before I took up golf course architecture, when it was an annual habit of mine to visit and play over some of the seaside courses in Great Britain. There the dunes were so much a part of the golf picture that I could not bring myself to visualize a course without looking at it through the irregular contours of sandy hillocks and the whins. These were traditional with the game itself, its origin and its growth.

Long Island, particularly out near its end, appeals to me as one of the most fortunate sections imaginable for golf course creation, or probably it would be much better to say—course development from natural creation. There you will find dunes

Photograph by Geoff Shackelford *(Old Tom Morris)*

A NATURAL BUNKER AT ROYAL COUNTY DOWN, NORTHERN IRELAND.

in plenty. As Findlay Douglas once remarked to me—"There are thousands of natural golf courses toward Montauk Point." And I know he was right.

But no doubt many of the hazard-shirking fraternity would declare that playing a wayward ball from such places was entirely too difficult. What utter nonsense! There were and are shots that will do it; another generation knew how to play them, and it is not altogether pleasant to think that golfers of today are going soft. Possibly a bit more sting in the rod of golf chastisement in these, our modern times, would render it more of an achievement to break par so habitually.

USGA *(Crump, Colt and Tillinghast)*

PINE VALLEY'S THIRTEENTH GREEN—MR. TILLINGHAST HAD A HAND IN DESIGNING THIS RUGGED AND NATURAL HOLE.

Photo by Geoff Shackelford *(Coore and Crenshaw)*

THE 450-YARD PAR-4 EIGHTEENTH AT SAND HILLS GOLF CLUB, MULLEN, NEBRASKA. A MODERN EXAMPLE OF IDEAL TERRAIN FOR GOLF.

No other game in the world has an architecture of a similar nature to boast of. A golf course, like a building, must have character and individuality because no one would be content with a mere reproduction. It is the same problem which confronts the architect of a house when he lays out the accessories and is continually adding new features as they suggest themselves. The plan very rarely is completed to accord exactly with the original intention. Walls, roofs, pillars, doors, windows, lawns and gardens are all of them elements capable of alteration in the same way that greens, fairways, hazards and the like admit of rearrangement. The difference is that golf has to do with a form of miniature and open warfare and is on that account subject to an underlying condition of strategy and tactics.

—H.N. Wethered and Tom Simpson

Part III

Planning, Construction, and Maintenance

Our third section provides several important essays for those fascinated by the elements which go into conceiving a golf course. Alister MacKenzie begins Part III by pleading to municipalities and those thinking about building a course to hire the services of a qualified architect, and he ends the section by discussing the problems incurred in remodeling courses when green committees want to get involved. William Flynn continues his distinctive explanation of creating a club in, "Designing the Course," his follow-up to the essays in Part II. William Langford, a relatively unknown but talented Chicago area architect from the 1920s, is featured with a short article from his architecture booklet. And Bobby Jones provides a shrewd explanation for soft greens and their ability to ruin the strategy of a well-designed hole.

~

Editor's Note
MacKenzie and Experts Needed

Golfdom Magazine was a 1920s and '30s trade publication that focused on the maintenance, construction, and design of golf courses. Created by Herb Graffis, who documented golf history for over forty years, *Golfdom* featured several MacKenzie articles after the doctor's move to California in 1925.

Many of the MacKenzie articles from *Golfdom* were merely excerpts from MacKenzie's *The Spirit of St. Andrews*, which was not published until 1995 after its discovery in a desk drawer by Ray Haddock, the doctor's step-grandson. Published posthumously, "Experts Needed" is an original and timeless MacKenzie essay.

In introducing "Experts Needed," Graffis wrote:

> One of the last articles written by the late Dr. Alister MacKenzie, internationally famed golf architect, is of timely interest because of extensive use of relief funds in municipal golf course construction. Dr. MacKenzie points out the great opportunity before municipal golf courses that are expertly designed and constructed. If his message were heeded by those responsible for the considerable amount of municipal course construction now being planned, use of public funds for such work would have the highest, practical justification.

Sounds like Mr. Graffis wrote this last week!

G.S.

~

Experts Needed:
Neglecting to Employ Qualified Architects Has Cost Thousands in Municipal Course Building

by Alister MacKenzie
Golfdom Magazine
February 1935

The more I know of golf and golf courses the more convinced I am of its influence on the health, the happiness and, owing to its effect on mental as well as physical fitness, the prosperity of the community.

One of the many advantages of capitalism is that under this system the luxuries of the rich today become the necessities of the poor tomorrow. This has been proved in regard to most things which at one time were the monopoly of the rich such as tea, coffee, sugar, automobiles, electric light, telephones, radios and even silk stockings, but golf and golf courses have fallen far behind other luxuries in this respect.

In olden days golf was the sport of kings, the Royal and Ancient game, but in Scotland in my youth, owing to the lessening in cost of clubs and balls, it became so popular that it was well within the reach of the artisan.

At the Braid Hills municipal course in Edinburgh and on many other municipal courses golf could be played for as little as three pence a round, and at St. Andrews the rate-payers and their families enjoy the game free of all cost.

In the United States often those in authority rarely appreciate the value of a golf course not only for its health-giving properties but also in providing wide open spaces free from buildings which are a permanent asset as the lungs of the city, and in the second place they fail to realize that a golf course which is well designed and constructed, invariably pays, and is not such a burden to the community in the form of taxes.

The natural conditions of soil and climate in America are not so suitable for providing golf courses at a low cost as in the home of golf, Scotland.

The chief cause of the comparatively high cost of golf, however, in the United States is due to the fact that the municipalities that intend on constructing a course rarely realize that the construction of a golf course is an extremely difficult art and if it is to attain its acme of popularity at a low cost of maintenance and construction it must be designed by an expert.

Build Right for Profit

Records show that a first-class golf architect designs a golf course at half the cost of construction charges and at a saving of at least 50 percent in maintenance charges under figures of an inferior architect. Moreover the course is twice as popular if computed in terms of green fees. This estimate of course is based on similar conditions of accessibility, nature of terrain and so on.

With the exception of cities like San Francisco and Sacramento that are blessed with Park Commissions and city managers of exceptional ability, cities are inclined to figure that if they get 9 or 18 holes of golf course they have handled the job properly. There never has and never will be an outstanding municipal golf course construction on these lines. The false economy of saving one or two thousand dollars in expert advice frequently leads to the loss of hundreds of thousands of dollars in increased cost of construction and maintenance and in deceased popularity as estimated in terms of green fees.

This may appear to be an exaggerated statement but I do not think that it is. I have in mind two public golf courses in the same city. One of them is less accessible and more unsuitable ground for golf than the other, but designed by an expert, whereas the other was designed by a man of extremely limited architectural experience. The one designed by a first-class architect has not cost half as much to construct and maintain and yet it gets $50,000 a year more in green fees than the other. Multiply this by the life of a golf course which may be 20 to 100 years (the old St. Andrews course, which is a municipal course, is over 300 years old) and the loss for the lack of expert advice may conceivably run into a million dollars or more.

There are a few general principles which apply to public courses even more than to private ones. It is of even greater importance than usual that the soil, climatic conditions and the nature of the water used for irrigation be carefully studied so as to select the most suitable seed and fertilizers to provide turf of hard wearing qualities.

A Civic Jewel

Beauty is of paramount importance. A municipal course designed by an architect who is an artist in constructing hillocks, hollows, sand bunkers, and the grouping of trees of a natural appearance, is almost invariably the beauty spot of the city. The most important thing of all in the designing and maintenance of a municipal course is the realization by everyone concerned that golf is played for fun, and that unless a golf course provides the maximum amount of pleasure for everyone, including the beginner who rarely gets a ball off the ground, it is not a complete success.

There should be no long grass or other hazard on a public course necessitating the annoyance and irritation of searching for lost balls, and there should be a minimum of sand bunkers.

On the other hand the course should be full of interesting features such as closely mown hillocks, hollows and swales creating fascinating strategic problems and making every hole of such a character that there is such infinite variety stimulating players to improve their games. Then the charm of the course grows and grows and grows so that golf never becomes stale.

The Old Course at St. Andrews in Scotland is an ideal public course in this respect. There is a constant stream of men, women and children playing on it all the year round from sunrise to sunset and yet it is such an excellent test of golf for a good player that Bobby Jones says he gets more pleasure in playing it than in a hundred other courses.

The course I made for Bobby Jones, the Augusta National, is similar to St. Andrews. There are only 22 sand traps on it. It is easy for the man who is content with fives and sixes and an occasional par, but it is extremely difficult for the golfer who is striving for sub-par figures. It is a private club but it would have made an ideal public golf course.

There is an old adage, "Penny wise and pound foolish," which applies as much to the laying-out and designing of golf courses as to anything else, but it requires men of vision to real-

Ralph W. Miller Golf Library *(Alister MacKenzie)*

OPENING DAY OF DR. MACKENZIE'S PASATIEMPO GOLF CLUB. THE GREEN IN THE FOREGROUND IS THE PAR-3 EIGHTH GREEN AND IN THE DISTANCE THE GLORIOUS PAR-5 NINTH.

ize this. Records show it however, and history has proved it. Beauty and finality must be provided for at the beginning, or the life of the course will be that of a cripple struggling along on crutches.

~

Editor's Note
Flynn and Designing the Course

The ultimate character of the course must be developed as the construction progresses. —William Flynn

A continuation of Flynn's previous two essays from Part II, "Designing the Course," was originally presented in two parts but is combined here into one edited version. In Part I, Flynn prescribes some of the main principles to be heeded when routing the course, including variety, the number of one-shotters to build, and the dilemma of the ever- increasing distance of the golf ball, or as Flynn calls it, that "elusive pill."

In Part II, Flynn emphasizes what appears to be the major problem with our modern day golf architecture: making modifications in the field. If you have ever wondered why some features of modern golf courses just do not look right, it's usually because the architect was not present often enough. The results are few on-site modifications as workers stick to written plans. He also discusses the tedious nature of copying famous holes in the construction of greens, and expresses interest in the development of bent grass which he felt made greens "slicker," thus requiring softer contours (Pete Dye gives a modern perspective of this issue in Part V). Flynn also discusses many elements of design strategy and bunker placement, and in general, pleads for architects to modify their bunker plans during construction to improve strategy.

Any observer who has studied Flynn's architectural counterparts and his influences from early twentieth-century Philadelphia, will recognize through "Designing the Course" that his philosophies virtually mirrored those of his mentors A.W. Tillinghast, George Thomas, Hugh Wilson and Pine Valley creator George Crump.

G.S.

~

Designing the Course—Parts I and II

by William Flynn
USGA Green Section Bulletin
August and September, 1927

Part I

When the architect has discussed with the club the type of course required, he is then free to proceed unhampered with the layout. In addition to the designing of the course he must consider the question of clubhouse site, parking area, practice ground, entrance roads, etc., because all these should coordinate with the course itself.

In order to get the best possible layout on any property the architect must have a topographical plan of the ground on which he is working. Following this he settles upon the clubhouse site and the starting and finishing points of the course around it, as well as the other necessary facilities. The most satisfactory layout in an 18-hole course today is the one which has two starting and two finishing points in close proximity to the clubhouse. The advantages of this plan are too well known to make it necessary to go into details.

A popular plan which is being widely inaugurated in newly formed clubs is to have three nine-hole loops radiating from the clubhouse. While a course of this kind will not accommodate as many players as a 36-hole course, yet it is capable of taking care of the play of most metropolitan clubs on busy days and gives a varied interchange of holes. In fact, it is possible to play six distinct 18-hole courses by changing the sequence of the various nines.

The character and quality of the course should naturally come first but it sometimes happens that a club has selected a property partly because a fine house was on the ground and could be readily adapted to the club needs. In a case of this kind the starting point of the course becomes fixed.

An ideal situation exists when such a spot overlooks the golf course and permits visibility of a large portion of the links as well as providing starting and finishing points as outlined above. In locating the clubhouse on a hill overlooking the course it is well to remember that while the getaway is easy, the return both at the ninth and eighteenth may possibly be severe from a climbing standpoint and care should be taken in selecting an eminence that provides gentle slopes at least for the return holes.

When the architect has determined the clubhouse site and his starting and finishing points for the golf course he then proceeds to find the holes for the course. While the procedure of all architects is not necessarily similar, yet they all work to the same end and the following is purely the method of one individual.

The most important point in designing golf holes is to select proper green sites. The first condition in selecting a green site is its adaptability to the game on a particular type of hole. The second is the question of the cost of constructing the green on any particular site. The third is the beauty to be had both in the background and vistas.

The finest layout in the world may lack interest if the surroundings are unpleasant, while the mediocre course appeals a great deal to the majority when the backgrounds and vistas are well thought out. It quite frequently happens that the architect will select perhaps 30 or 40 different green sites on a property when his ultimate job is to secure only 18. This is done to exhaust all the possibilities of securing good holes. It often occurs that an architect lays out perhaps three different courses on paper before he definitely decides which, in his estimation, is best.

Contrary to the way the course is played, that is from tee to green, the architect selects his greens first and then works backward to his tees radiating in all directions from the green until he eventually secures what he is after. The principal thought in designing a course is to produce 18 interesting holes with variety of play. A course which has variety of play and character in its natural state can readily be made even more interesting by the installation of a limited number of man-made hazards.

When the architect selects a suitable spot for a green site he marks it on the contour plan which he always carries in the field. All the while he is making notes on the topographical map and in his notebook as to the character of the ground, drainage, size of trees, and all sorts of points that will enter into the cost of construction.

When he has made a complete study of the ground and exhausted all the possibilities of green locations, etc., he takes his marked plan back to his drafting room and then with his notes ties in the various green sites. During the tying in process the architect always has in mind the question of the sequence of the various types, taking care not to have holes of similar length and character coming too closely together. The most interesting course is one where the lengths and types of holes are broken up, where two or three drive and pitch holes or any other type for that matter do not follow each other.

USGA Green Section Bulletin *(Crump and Colt)*

THE SHORT BUT "DEVILISH" PAR-3 TENTH AT PINE VALLEY. MR. FLYNN WAS VERY INVOLVED WITH MODIFICATION TO PINE VALLEY IN THE EARLY YEARS OF ITS EXISTENCE.

Perhaps the majority of players enjoy the one-shot holes on any course better than the longer ones and the architect should be careful to get distinctive short holes of the proper length. The principal thought in mind is to fit the best possible holes to the ground and while the custom is to have four short holes there is no reason why this number should not be reduced to three or increased to five if conditions warrant it.

The question as to the number of the various types of two and three-shot holes for a course is one that has created a great deal of discussion in the past and this will continue as long as the game is played, but more on this later.

Unlike most other games, golf has no definitely prescribed area over which the game shall be played. While in the past 10 years or more the yardage held up as being suitable for a "championship" course ranged between 6,000 to 6,500 yards, this year's open championship was decided on a course approximately 7,000 yards long. But all courses can not be "championship" courses, that is, links where championships are decided, for they would be too expensive for the average club.

It should be the aim of the architect to lay out his course in such a way as to get the proper length holes at the proper places. Actual yardage, however is not the determining factor in this or that type of hole, for a 430-yard hole down the hill may very easily be a drive and mashie niblick while a hole reversed on similar ground might be two full wood shots.

Again the question of the ball has a great bearing on what type a certain length hole will be. Time was, and not so many years ago, when a hole 400 yards long on average ground was a good two-shot hole for the star players; now, the same hole is perhaps a drive and spade for the better class golfers.

In view of this, the architect of today plans his full two-shot holes from 440 yards to 500 yards, depending on the character of the land and if the distance to be obtained with the ball continues to increase, it will be necessary to increase the length of all holes on golf courses accordingly if the same standards of play are to be maintained.

All architects will be a lot more comfortable when the powers that be in golf finally solve the ball problem. A great deal of experimentation is now going on and it is to be hoped that before long a solution will be found to control the distance of the elusive pill.

If, as in the past, the distance to be gotten with the ball continues to increase, it will be necessary to go to 7,500 and even 8,000 yard courses, and more yards mean more money for the golfer to fork out.

In addition to getting the proper length and sequence of holes in the layout the architect should be careful to leave sufficient room between the various fairways. When there is continued paralleling of fairways there is not as much chance to segregate holes as in the triangulating method of design.

The question of handling galleries must be considered in designing the present-day championship course, and ample room must be allowed to take care of the tremendous crowds that mill back and forth following their favorites.

Many times the less the prominent players, particularly in medal competitions, have been completely thrown off their game by the crowd following the favorite overflowing or rushing to gain advantage point and thus greatly hampering those just behind or in front. Having plotted a layout on paper after having given all the above points due consideration the architect now has a preliminary plan which is ready for the engineer to stake on the ground.

Part II

In staking the preliminary layout of the golf course on the ground the first thing the architect's engineer does is locate the center of each tee, green and the angle, if there happens to be one, on the various holes. The staking is done so that the architect may check up and revise any particular site where necessary. It often happens that swinging a hole slightly to the right or left eliminates the necessity of drilling and excavating rock. Serious drainage conditions may be obviated by the slight shifting of a green or tee. It often happens that a layout planned on paper does not exactly stake out where the architect thought it would and it is necessary to make a very careful check of the site for greens and tees. It might also be that moving a tee slightly to the right or left precludes the necessity of taking out some beautiful trees. This also applies to green sites. Sometimes a slight change in the alignment of the hole permits the architect to keep a specimen tree or trees which also may act as a key or turning point in the hole. In making minor revisions as outlined above it does not necessarily follow that the character of the course is in any way changed. As a matter of fact it generally improves the layout.

In connection with the design of the greens it is very desirable to have a close survey or cross section of each green site, say 100 feet square, showing one-foot contours. With this type of survey the architect can then design a green that will fit into its particular location, making it blend with the surroundings and presenting a natural effect.

There has been in the past considerable copying in the designs of greens. The custom has been to select so-called famous holes from abroad and attempt to adapt them to a particular hole. While it is a simple matter to copy a design it is almost impossible to turn out a green that resembles the original. This is not due to any technical reason but is on account of the surroundings being different from the original.

Copying greens in detail is not generally a good plan but there should be no hesitation about copying the principle connected with any green, particularly when it is good. It has often been said that architects have designs for 18 greens and that the same ones are used over and over again on the various layouts. A successful architect of today does not follow that system. His greens are born on the ground and made to fit each particular hole.

In constantly designing greens it is very easy for an architect to acquire a pet type and to apply this frequently, thus creating greens of great similarity. A tremendous amount of study must be given each site on the ground and also on paper so as to get distinctive types, thus avoiding sameness.

The length of the shot to the green as well as the bunkering scheme of the hole must be considered in the design of each green. A green receiving a long iron shot should not have the same gradient or be of the same size as a green receiving a mashie, niblick or a brassy shot. Care must be taken so that in the main body of the green there shall be sufficient cup space, a very important consideration when the wear and tear of the green is considered, as limited cup area increases wear.

The tendency in the past ten years has been to bank up greens to a greater degree than is really necessary. While holes with long second shots, whether iron or wood, should have a reasonable amount of rise, yet the value of being able to apply stop or under spin to a shot is entirely lost when such a condition prevails with a mashie or mashie niblick to the green.

The advent of vegetatively planted creeping bent in a measure checked this condition. This is due to the fact that the bent creates a more uniform surface and mowers have been improved, thus giving us a faster green or one that is in tournament condition all the time rather than, as in the past, merely during the running of a competition.

Steep slopes are out of the question, particularly in the main body of a vegetatively planted green. In the old days the mixed seed greens were cut down real close only when an important tournament was being played. At that time the word "slippery" was often used in connection with a description of the greens. If we still keep steep slopes with our vegetative greens we will keep on hearing the expression "slippery."

USGA Green Section Bulletin *(Wilson and Flynn)*

THE PAR-3 NINTH AT MERION GOLF CLUB (EAST).

The most important consideration in conjunction with the designing of a green is to create naturalness. Of course this condition can only be brought about as construction progresses, but the frame work must be right in the beginning. Naturalness should apply on all construction on golf courses, greens, tees, mounds and bunkers alike. It is much more expensive to construct a natural looking golf course on account of the tremendous amount of material that must be moved, but the money saved in the subsequent maintenance greatly offsets the original cost.

In designing greens the architect not only makes a close-up study of the green sites but also studies from a distance, that is from the spot where the shot to the green is supposed to be played. Having visibility of the green surface from this point is one of the most important considerations in the design of a golf course. The drive, with the exception of the carry or accuracy required, is practically similar on each hole and securing visibility of the area played to is not nearly as important as securing visibility for the shot to the green on any type hole. The green is the final objective and how can a man reach the objective satisfactorily if he can not see it?

It naturally follows that any bunker construction in conjunction with the greens should also be visible. However, it is not always possible to have visibility of every green but the hole that does not have a visible green should have some other feature or indicator which tells the player where to go to get the best results. Visibility in the shot to the green is much to be desired and a little more time spent in modifying the layout may perhaps bring about the result desired and increase the pleasure in the play of the course.

The design for bunkering the course is tremendously important and the architect should spend a great deal of time going over various holes determining the exact location of his fairway bunkers. It is important in locating fairway bunkers to place them in positions where they are also visible. The best looking bunkers are those that are gouged out of faces or slopes, particularly when the slope faces the player. They are very much more effective in that they stand out like sentinels beckoning the player to come on or keep to the right or left.

A very important consideration in the design of bunkers is to make each one surface drain. In flat country this condition can be secured by building them above the surface of the surrounding terrain. It is not wise to attempt to design a complete bunkering system for the course in the beginning but the frame work bunkering plan can be worked out and as the course is played a complete scheme developed more satisfactorily and to better advantage.

The placing of the tees requires considerable thought and they also should be designed to fit in and blend with the landscape. The topography of the ground should have a bearing in the outlining of the fairways, they being designed with the idea of producing character rather than the commonplace straight line effect of a decade ago. A curving line whether it be a road or the outline of a fairway is much more attractive than the straight line.

After a complete study of the whole course in the preliminary layout the architect takes his plan again back to his office or drafting room to make his final general layout plan. In conjunction with the plans the architect must prepare specifications for the construction of the course. While the specifications for golf course construction are generally similar, yet there are seldom two courses alike and the architect must consider any peculiarities that may occur in a particular course and take care of them accordingly.

Although the architect has spent a great deal of time and study in the preparing of the plans only the frame work has been finished. The ultimate character of the course must be developed as the construction progresses.

~

Editor's Note
William Langford and Architecture

A standout player who played on three NCAA Championship teams at Yale and reached the semifinals of the U.S. Amateur, William Langford was an underrated designer of courses throughout the Midwest. Educated as an engineer, he formed a partnership with Theodore Moreau in 1918 that lasted thirty years. The team of Langford and Moreau focused much of their work in the Midwest and Florida. Much like the dynamic duos of Flynn and Toomey or Thomas and Bell, Langford was the strategist and salesman while Moreau handled the engineering duties.

Similar to his counterparts during the 1920s and '30s, Langford was a strategic designer who emphasized the short game with boldly undulating greens and deep, grass-faced bunkering. He designed or remodeled some 250 courses during his career, and later on, even redesigned some of his own courses because of changes in equipment and fears that his courses would become obsolete.

Langford's design at Wakonda Club in Iowa and redesign work at Skokie Country Club in Illinois remain as his most acclaimed. He wrote several fine essays in what amounted to be his design brochure. Entitled "Golf Course Architecture in the Chicago Golf District," Langford focuses most of his thoughts on construction, and suggests various methods to build more cost-effective designs while maintaining enough interest to create a fine course.

In Langford's "Placing Hazards," reference is made to John L. Low of Scotland. Low became acquainted with many of golf's important architects when he helped form the Oxford and Cambridge Golfing Societies. Among the early members of those organizations were future master architects C.H. Alison and H.S. Colt.

Low was the first person to actually write about the principles of course architecture in his 1903 book, *Concerning Golf*. It is safe to say, based on the number of references to Low made by everyone from MacKenzie to Langford, that his architecture principles became the building blocks for the great architects of the "Golden Age of Golf Design."

A sampling of Low's philosophy, as summarized by Ron Whitten and Geoffrey Cornish in their seminal work, *The Architects of Golf*:

- A golf course should provide entertainment for the high and medium handicapper while at the same time present a searching and difficult test for the accomplished golfer.
- The shortest, most direct line to the hole, even if it be the center of the fairway, should be fraught with danger.
- The architect must allow the ground to dictate play. The good architect sees that there is a special interest for the accomplished golfer in each stroke, just as a billiard player always has in mind the next stroke or strokes.
- A course should never pretend to be, not is it intended to be, an infallible tribunal of skill alone. The element of chance is the very essence of the game, part of the fun of the game.

In Langford's concise description of placing hazards, the simplicity of good strategic golf course design is revealed. The most novice of architecture students will understand Langford's explanation. Not only does he provide excellent sketches to prove his point, Langford lets the simplicity of the holes prove his point that strategic holes are not as difficult to build as many modern architects seem to think.

G.S.

~

Placing Hazards

by William Langford

Golf Course Architecture in the Chicago Golf District

1915

Hazards should not be built solely with the idea of penalizing bad play, but with the object of encouraging thoughtful golf and of rewarding the player who possesses the ability to play a variety of strokes with each club. John L. Low has said that no hazard is unfair wherever placed, and while this is true, a hazard is obviously the wrong place to play one's shot, yet the proper placing of hazards will bring about very much more interesting golf than a haphazard arrangement of them is apt to do.

Topographical features may arbitrarily determine the location of hazards on a hole, and if the ground is at all rolling, will certainly influence the bunkering system to a large extent. As the number of topographical combinations is infinite, so is the possible arrangement of hazards on holes of any given length. The only general statement that can be made is this: hazards should be placed so that any player can avoid them if he gauges his ability correctly, so that they will make every man's game more interesting, no matter what class player he is, and offer a reward commensurate with the player's ability.

The accompanying sketches are attempts to show hazards arranged according to this principle. The dotted lines show the course taken by the ball.

Figure 1 shows a water hazard, exacting but fair to all players. Figure 2 shows five ways of playing the same hole, at least

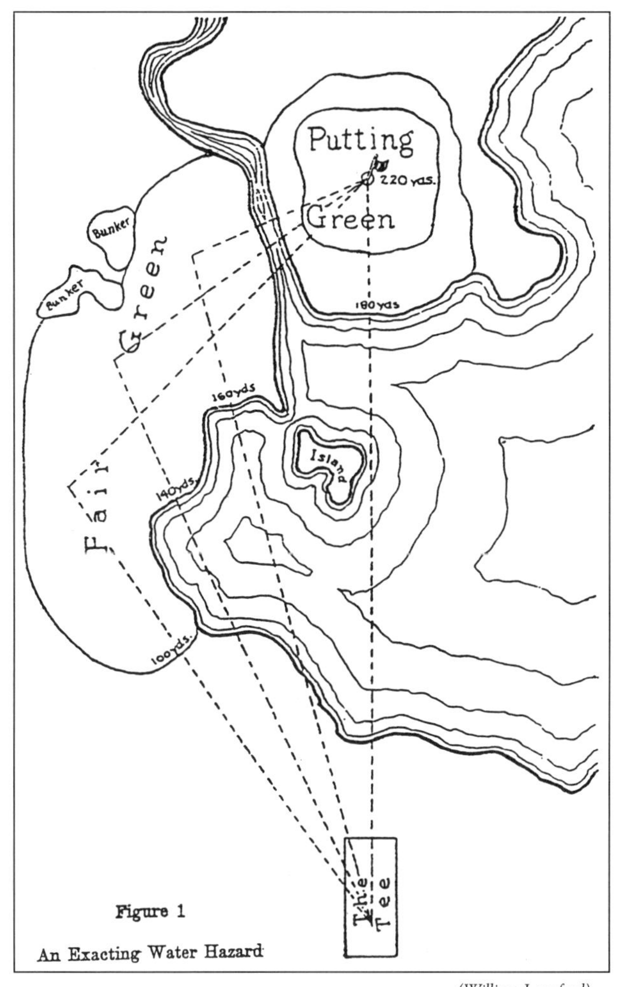

(William Langford)

FIGURE 1 - AN EXACTING WATER HAZARD.

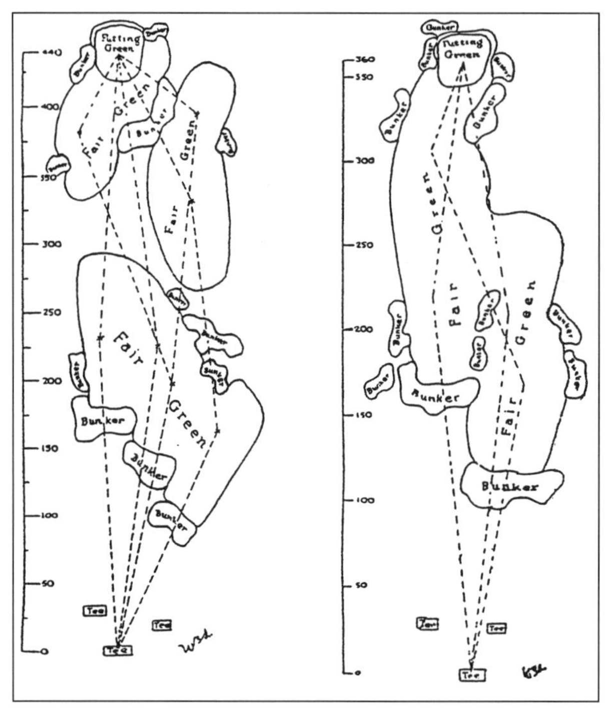

(William Langford)

FIGURE 2 (LEFT) - SHOWING FIVE WAYS OF PLAYING THE SAME HOLE.
FIGURE 3 (RIGHT) - THIS SKETCH SHOWS A HOLE WITH TWO AVENUES OF PLAY.

one of which is well within the ability of any golfer. The echelon arrangement of bunkers for the tee shot allows three carries of widely varying length. The second shot bunkers are placed so as to offer a reward proportionate to the risk taken at the tee. Figure 3 shows a hole with two avenues of play, one for the short driver, one for the long. He who chooses the short carry from the tee is confronted with a very difficult second to the green; he who successfully negotiates the long carry is rewarded by an open approach. Figure 4 depicts a bottle-neck hole demanding extreme accuracy.

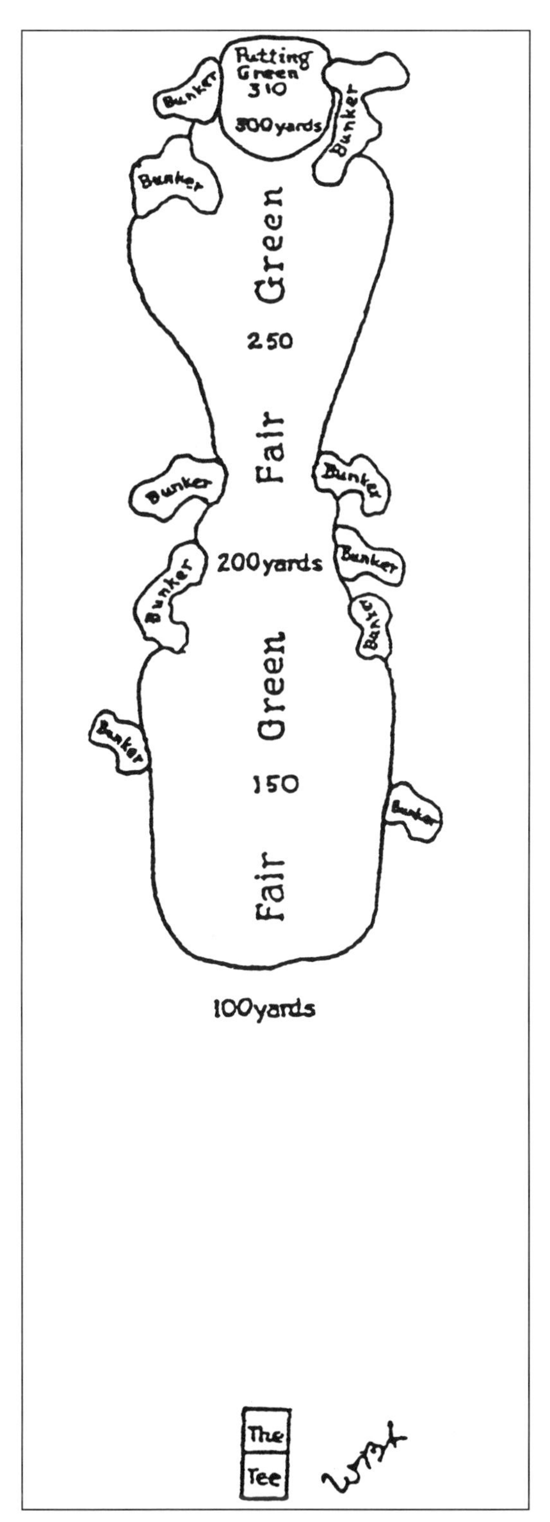

(William Langford)

FIGURE 4 - BOTTLE NECK HOLE DEMANDING ACCURACY.

~

Editor's Note
Bobby Jones and Soft Greens

The "greatest of them all," Bobby Jones, left us with a wealth of golfing wisdom both in the form of an extensive collection of written work and his classic film series. Jones was an extraordinary writer, able to express his thoughts in a remarkably concise and clear manner. Though most of his writing dealt with the golf swing and the mental side of the game, Jones did write an occasional piece on architecture.

A favorite topic for Jones was the debate over soft greens and their ability to ruin a strategically sound hole. Later in his life, Jones wrote of his dismay over the evolution of the British Isles courses where soft conditions had become more prevalent. He responded to Pat Ward-Thomas in 1961 about changes Thomas had informed him of: "I cannot help being saddened by what you tell me of the changes in turf conditions at Lytham. I know I was shocked to observe the same changes at St. Andrews. If this sort of thing is happening to all British seaside golf, then indeed, progress has been dearly bought."

Written not long after his retirement and during the construction of Augusta National, "Why Keep Putting Green's Soft?" is Jones' kindlier, more diplomatic explanation of why spongy greens create poorer golfers and defenseless courses. One can only imagine how pleased Jones would be to see that his dream course, Augusta National, still presents firm greens every year at the Masters, thus preserving the strategy of its design.

G.S.

~

Why Keep Putting Greens Soft?

by Robert Tyre Jones, Jr.
USGA Green Section Bulletin
February 1932

It is claimed by those in close touch with greenkeeping practices that much of the difficulty in maintaining putting greens is due to the excessive use of water and that greenkeepers and green committees point out that they water heavily in self-defense because golfers want soft greens. I have been asked to say how I regard the practice of keeping putting surfaces soft, even soggy, looking at the question purely from the player's standpoint.

There can be little question that the great mass of golfers in the United States prefer their greens very soft. Such a condition makes the play much easier for all classes of players and is, in a great measure, responsible for the fact that tournament scoring is uniformly lower in the United States than on seaside links in the British Isles. The difference is attributable more to the excessive use of water on putting greens in the United States than to the much-talked-of seaside gales in the British Isles, which, after all do not blow constantly.

Of our two great American preferences—the one for placing the green bunkering very close to the putting surfaces, and the other for soggy greens which will hold any kind of pitch, whether struck with backspin or not—I can not say which induced the other or which came first. The close guarding, in many instances, makes a soft green necessary if the hole is to be playable, and easy pitching, on the other hand, makes it necessary to decrease the size of the target in order to supply any test.

I quarrel with both ends of this proposition, whichever is to blame. These together are the two reasons, I think, why our golf courses in the main lack the subtlety of the British links, and why our golf does not demand the strategy or the intelligent planning it should. In my opinion, a properly designed hole should impose a test upon each shot which the player has to make. There should always be a definite advantage to be gained from an accurate and intelligent placing of the tee shot, or a reward offered for a long, well-directed carry over some obstacle. This advantage or reward can be only in the shape of an easier and more open road for the second shot, and when we soak the green with water we absolutely nullify the advantage which the design of the hole has held out.

I do not believe in forcing a run-up shot in preference to a pitch in every case. But, when one goes to the trouble of placing a bunker across the left side of the green in order to force the tee shot toward the right side of the fairway, why destroy its effect by soaking the green so that any sort of pitch over the bunker will hold? Our expert players are in the habit of playing long iron, spoon, and brassy shots bang up to the hole. As long as they can do this no architect can expect them to worry much about placing the tee shots.

It seems to me that the ideal green would be sufficiently soft to hold only a properly placed pitch—and by "hold" I do not mean "to stay within a very few feet." To carry out the intention of the designer, conditions ought to be such that a definite penalty should be sustained by the player who has played himself out of position.

In this connection, I think one of our greatest needs is a fairway grass or treatment which will make the ground in front of our putting greens more reliable. If the greens themselves are maintained in a firmer condition, the need must arise on occasions to drop the ball short of the putting surface, allowing it to roll the remaining distance. I know very few courses where this is possible without great uncertainty.

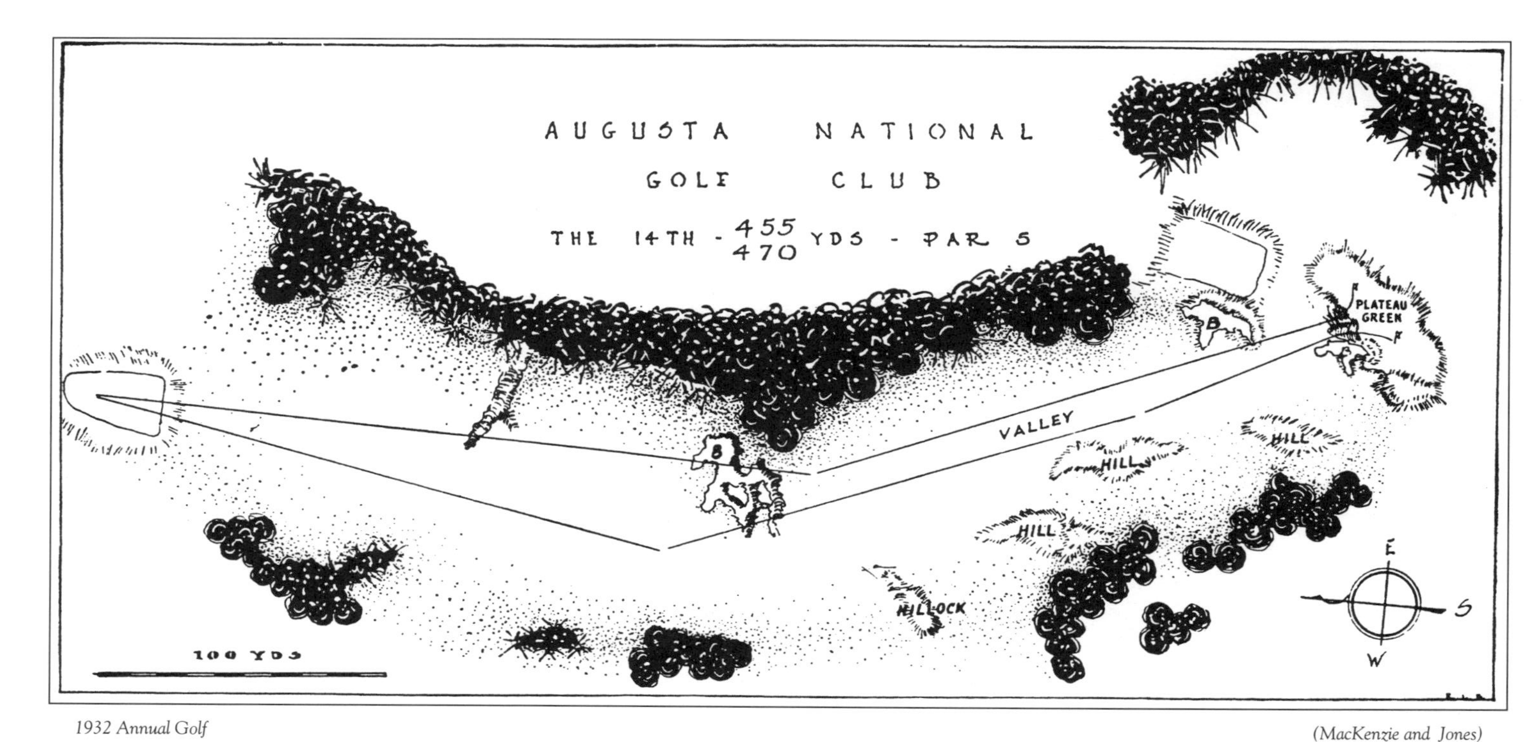

1932 Annual Golf *(MacKenzie and Jones)*

DR. MACKENZIE'S ORIGINAL SKETCH OF TODAY'S FIFTH HOLE AT AUGUSTA NATIONAL. IMAGINE HOW THE STRATEGY OF THIS HOLE CHANGES WITH A SOFT GREEN. MR. JONES DESCRIBED THE HOLE : "THIS IS A SIMILAR HOLE TO THE FAMOUS SEVENTEENTH ROAD HOLE AT ST. ANDREWS, SCOTLAND. THE GREEN IS ON A PLATEAU AND THE PLAYER WHO HUGS THE TREES (INDICATED IN BLACK ON MAP) HAS A VISIBLE SHOT, THE PLAYER WHO AVOIDS THE WOODS AND STEERS WIDE OF THE BUNKERS (B) HAS A BLIND APPROACH."

~

Editor's Note
MacKenzie and Green Committees

Alister MacKenzie could rarely write for more than a few pages without returning to the subject of green committees who have ruined courses or committees, who for unknown reasons, want to redesign their course. Though some have felt that MacKenzie went too far in his assessments of the average committee member, I generally have to agree with the doctor's appraisal.

I have sat on the Green Committee at my home course, and at each monthly meeting I am always amazed at the ridiculous suggestions made by some of the committee members who have absolutely no expertise in the areas we are discussing. Often times, I will suggest that we need to get the advice of an expert and almost always that concept is met with disdain by those with no clue about the subject at hand.

Another subject MacKenzie addresses in "Remodeling Courses" is the problem of committees making changes just for the sake of leaving their mark on the course. There is one very wonderful old course in my hometown that has been so badly butchered by committees over the years that I honestly feel it would make the original architect sick to his stomach if he saw it today. And why are the changes made? To get the course to a so-called "Championship" yardage so they have something to brag about. Meanwhile, it is now completely devoid of charm, strategy or character.

G.S.

~

Problems in Remodeling Courses

by Alister MacKenzie
The American Golfer
May 1933

It is a rather extraordinary thing that members of golf committees, themselves men of intelligence, experience and frequently specialists in different lines, when it comes to consideration of the task involved in remodeling the club course, will turn to seek the advice of persons whose only qualification in matters pertaining to golf is the ability to play a good game. Granted that the play of such persons is probably a fitting measure by which to judge the merit of a course, the fact still remains that worthwhile course designing is a matter for specialists in that line. And the stature of the specialist is determined by the character of work which he has turned out.

The mere fact that a course is considered to require alteration should be a warning that unless the committee is very careful, the club may make the same mistakes again, and every precaution should be taken to ensure that any changes to be made shall be of a permanent and lasting character. After all, the cost of expert advice is infinitesimal compared with the cost of manual labor and particularly unproductive manual labor.

The so-called improvements of golf courses usually consist of making holes longer and in riddling the place with sand bunkers. If a hole is uninteresting to start with, it can only be made more so by lengthening it, and most golf courses have too many sand traps already.

As a rule, it is surprisingly difficult to obtain the cooperation of club members in agreeing to the advice of an expert, except on the foolish pretense that changes in the ball or the addition of new traps make it desirable to bring the course up to date. I have a vivid recollection of an occasion over thirty years ago, when the president of a club to which I belonged addressed the members and stated that the introduction of the rubber-cored ball made it necessary to lengthen the course. He added that he proposed to make it the world's best golf course by lengthening it to 7,000 yards. He succeeded in making it the worst, and it was not until, under expert advice, they shortened it by a thousand yards that it regained its popularity.

It is remarkable how loyal the ordinary club member is to his own course. His friends play there and he has many pleasant recollections of enjoyable rounds with them. The course may be so bad that he gets tired of golf without realizing the reason why, and sometimes he either gives up the game altogether or wanders off to "pastures new." He may submit to changes made by the greens committee, but he will rarely admit openly that his course is not all that it should be by submitting it to outside expert advice.

There are rare instances of chairmen of greens committees who have made a lifelong study of golf architecture as was the case of the late John L. Low at Woking in England and the Wilson brothers at the Merion Cricket Club in America. But in the majority of cases, changes made by the green committee consist in the construction of more penal hazards and the making of the course even less interesting than it was before.

The majority of green committees consist of men averaging from four to twelve handicap and they are usually subconsciously influenced against any handicap or hazard which will penalize themselves, but are unanimous in agreeing to the introduction of new hazards which will make the life of the long-handicap player a living purgatory. They rarely have the grasp and conception of Bobby Jones, who agreed most emphatically in the case of the Augusta National that due consideration was to be given the high-handicap player in all cases, but that the course must be made so difficult for himself that he would be continually striving for shots he has hitherto been unable to do. The result of our consultations at the Augusta National was to reduce the number of sand traps on the plan from thirty-six to twenty-two.

Few committees appear to realize that after all golf is played for fun, and that the most important thing in reconstructing a golf course is to make it more pleasurable. The most successful committees are those who are ruled by a benevolent autocrat, who has made a life-long study of the requirements of golf. I have done most of my reconstruction work for men of this kind; men who know golf, but realize that they had no sufficient knowledge to know about everything, and who consequently were only too anxious to consult anyone who might throw fresh light on their problems.

I have recently had two striking examples of this. In both instances the ruling autocrat had already made considerable improvements in the course and had gained the confidence of the members.

One example was the Palmetto Golf Course at Aiken in South Carolina. The chairman, owing to the strength and endearing quality of his personality, managed to push things through notwithstanding the opposition of perhaps four-fifths of the members, and called me in to reconstruct the course. The alterations have been such a success that the chairman of Bobby Jones' executive committee at the Augusta National writes to me saying "We have only one serious complaint to make against you regarding the Augusta National. That layout you designed at Aiken is liked so well that the Aiken colony do not seem to be the least bit interested in coming over to the Augusta National."

The other instance concerned a club among the oldest in America. The course was designed years before anyone had formulated any definite ideas about golf architecture, so it was hardly to be expected that the layout would be ideal. As a matter of fact, the general design was no better than that of other courses which were constructed about the same period.

The first four and the last four holes were extremely hilly. There were many fine architectural features and backgrounds which were not utilized. There were many parallel holes and there was a stream, which should have been used as a diagonal hazard, which was crossed at right angles. Their course was far too difficult for the average golfer, and, on the other hand, of little interest to the good player. In fact it was somewhat surprising that the members got any real pleasure in playing it.

On the other hand the chairman of the green committee had made a study of golf courses, and had eliminated the worst of the hill climbing at the end of the course. Also the club had an excellent greenskeeper, who had got the greens into very good shape. Apart from the hills, there was not much acreage to make a first class golf course and a plan for taking in more ground involving an expenditure of considerably more than a hundred thousand dollars had been considered.

My problem was to use as many of the existing greens as possible and to evolve a good golf course at a minimum of expense. I had never had a more difficult problem with which to deal, and, after several weeks of careful study and planning, I evolved a scheme which, without taking in any additional land,

The American Golfer (Alister MacKenzie)

A GREEN UNDER CONSTRUCTION.

The American Golfer

THE COMPLETED CONSTRUCTION.

(Alister MacKenzie)

would give an exceptionally pleasurable and interesting course at an extremely low cost. One hole had already been made from one of the plans, when unfortunately something happened in the inner workings of the club, and the work was not carried through to a finish.

I had a somewhat similar case in Montreal. The green committee accepted plans for the reconstruction, but the directors, fearing that we should make the course too difficult, over-ruled their decision. They little appreciated that the plan would have eliminated more than half their penal hazards and have made the course infinitely more interesting and enjoyable.

There is another most important point about the reconstruction of golf courses. If the work is done on what we consider the right lines, namely eliminating all purely penal hazards and grading all the slopes so that they are of such a natural appearance that little or no hand labor is required in taking care of them, the cost of reconstruction is practically nothing, in the long run.

I have been informed by the chairmen of both the Lake Merced and the California clubs in San Francisco whose courses I reconstructed, that we have saved the clubs the whole of the cost of reconstruction in reducing maintenance every year since the remodeling was carried out. I have also been informed that these clubs have continued to increase their memberships and have consequently increased in prosperity in spite of the prevailing conditions.

Remodeling and reconstruction which results in added pleasure in the play of the club members and their friends, is very much worthwhile. The result is added interest on the part of old members and the attracting of new ones. A job which fails in doing that is nothing more than money thrown away and is as well left undone.

Pacific Coast Golfer *(Alister MacKenzie)*

THE SEVENTEENTH AT LAKE MERCED GOLF CLUB, CALIFORNIA, AFTER DR. MACKENZIE'S REMODELING.

~

Then, again, a golf course is a field of manoeuvre and action, employing, as it were, the military and engineering side of the game. It opens up a series of tactical and strategical opportunities, the implications of which it would be well for every golfer to grasp, whether he happens to approve or disapprove of the conclusions we have ventured to put forward. It is important to emphasize the necessity for the golfer to use his head as much as his hands; or, in other words, to make his mental agility match his physical ability.

—H.N. Wethered and Tom Simpson

~

Part IV

Hazards and Holes

Hazards and Holes provides a change of pace from the general principles of architecture and construction. Part IV celebrates the most interesting aspects of course design, ranging from a celebration of one-shotters to essays about the placing of hazards.

A.W. Tillinghast opens our fourth section with what many consider to be the defining essay of his vast collection, "Giving Individuality to Golf Holes." Robert Hunter returns to explain "The Purpose of Hazards," an exploration that prepares us for essays by George Thomas and Alister MacKenzie. Thomas writes about his favorite hole to build and design: par-3s. C.B. Macdonald and H.J. Whigham go a step further and elaborate on their favorite type of par-3, the Redan.

After our two articles on one-shotters, Dr. MacKenzie clarifies how "Water Holes Should Tempt, Not Torture," another posthumously published essay. Next is A.W. Tillinghast's succinct complaint about "The Fetish of Length," and Part IV concludes with Bernard Darwin's "Who Wants the Course Made Harder?," a wonderful look at architecture, the need for difficulty, and green committees.

~

Editor's Note
Tillinghast and Variety

The five primary members of the "Philadelphia School of Design" (George Crump, Hugh Wilson, George Thomas, William Flynn, and A.W. Tillinghast) all stressed certain design principles, whether it be perceived through their work or read in their essays. The standards that constituted a design by one of the Philadelphians could best be summed up in the following list: variety, strategy, naturalness, beauty, and individuality.

In "Giving Individuality to Golf Holes," A.W. Tillinghast uses, of all topics, the naming of golf holes as a premise for prescribing his design principles. Do not be fooled by the preliminary text on Tillinghast's desire to name holes in order to bequeath some individuality upon them. He proceeds to cover the architectural elements of variety, strategy, beauty, and a favorite of 1920s architects: green committees.

Like so many of the architects featured in this book, Tillinghast was more than a fine writer; he was a brilliant creator of courses. Esteemed golf historian and retired USGA executive Frank Hannigan summed up "Tillie's" fieldwork in the reprinted edition of Tillinghast's fictional books:

> Tillinghast's primary assets as an architect were his roving mind, rich imagination and sense of aesthetics. He believed in variety; the converse of the appalling modern trick of imposing on the property one or more gimmicks linked to the architect, e.g. railroad ties or "collection" bunkers. He did not say, "See, this is all about me." Thus, Winged Foot is not recognizable as having been created by the same man who turned out Baltusrol.

G.S.

~

Giving Individuality to Golf Holes

by A.W. Tillinghast
Golf Illustrated
January 1923

Any theatrical producer will tell you that the successful performer must possess talent primarily, and to an almost equal degree, personality. Without an appealing personality, a magnetism which draws the audience across the footlights, the actor must be endowed with rare ability to "get his stuff over"—as they say. But with talent, plus personality, the reward of spontaneous, sincere applause is assured. A salesman of any commodity may offer for trade, wares of undoubted excellence, but if he lacks the faculty of making the buyer like him personally he will find it hard sledding to market his merchandise. A wholesome, inspiring individuality goes a long way yet to make the man. The golf hole should have it just the same as a human.

For no good reason the green committees throughout the country ceased nominating the holes other than by numbers, and to many it seemed that the units of our courses had fallen from the caste of gentility to that of the criminal. Good, honest John Mann might just as suddenly have become convict 41144, and with as little cause, as did (let us say, for example) the famous Arena when the scorecards, possibly with ink saving excuse, gave it a number, and robbed of its good name, the fine old hole became plain Sixteen, and dragged through the years in lock-step with the others. There were good reasons for calling the hole Arena, and there was none other like it. Everywhere golfers knew of its renown, and many could tell you of the beauties of the hole itself, yet might hesitate in the naming of the course which contained it. As Sixteen it lost much of its identity, and became one of many sixteens.

In the last few years the naming of holes is becoming general, and certainly the return of the old custom is welcome. However, there should be some real and appropriate reason for bestowing of a name. It may be recalled, with almost as little reason in the old days Westward Ho! was tagged at the first opportunity to a hole shooting into the west, although it was bad enough to play a sun-hole without calling attention to the fact that it pointed in a mighty mean direction. There should be names for golf holes, but let them be significant and unique. The plains Indians never named their children until some incident in the child's life suggested a fitting one. Frequently the real name waited until the individual was advanced in youth, or even a warrior, as was the case with Plenty Coups and Young Man Afraid of His Horses. Not that we might pattern the names of golf holes after the red men in fact, but there must be some outstanding feature or incident that will give to a hole an individuality that none other may enjoy. This brings me to the real point of my article by possibly a devious path.

Let every hole be worthy of a name. If it does not possess a striking individuality through some gift of Nature, it must be given as much as possible artificially, and the artifice must be introduced in so subtle a manner as to make it seem natural. The photograph of the Elm holes shows one to which a name fastened itself immediately. Often a hole will name itself as this one did. The fine elm beyond the green lends a charming indi-

Golf Illustrated *(A. W. Tillinghast)*

ILLUSTRATING THE CHARACTER WHICH IS GIVEN BY THE TREATMENT OF SUCH A FEATURE. BEARING THE COGNOMEN OF THE "ELM," THIS HOLE ON WINGED FOOT'S WEST COURSE HAS GAINED A SIGNIFICANCE THROUGH ITS NAME WHICH IT OTHERWISE MIGHT NOT ENJOY.

viduality to the hole, which would have been totally missing had this tree been felled. Yet the surroundings of the green in the virgin state presented nothing of the present effect. As a matter of fact, there were many trees at this place—most of them worthless, to be sure, but quite sufficient to hide most of the beauty of the splendid specimen that stands alone, its solitary vigil suggesting a sentinel, which by the way might have been an equally appropriate name. Probably it is a good example of lending dignity to a hole with the aid of Nature. In my humble opinion the smaller companion elm, which was removed, would have destroyed the beauty in this particular instance.

Often a name will attach itself, and did so even in the days when numbers were used almost exclusively. This was a fact at

Shawnee, which course I had the honor of planning. There the present sixteenth has never been known by any appellation other than the Binniekill. This hole is individual to a marked degree, and it is almost entirely natural. The shot is ordinarily a mashie and entirely across water, which otherwise would have been commonplace. Certainly there are better holes at Shawnee than the Binniekill, but not one remains longer in the memory of the golfing pilgrim than this wee one which happens at such a fortunate time in the round; for there is no better place for a good short hole than at the sixteenth when the close match is drawing to its end and nerves are taut with accuracy at a tremendous premium.

This reference to the unusual appeal and individuality of a good water hazard warrants the inclusion of a particularly fine photograph of one of the new holes of the Winged Foot Golf Club of the New York Athletic Club at Mamaroneck, in Westchester County, New York. This has been christened Old Soak, for reasons which are obvious. It is worthy of brief description, since the natural features are unusual and impressive. In the first place, two separate lakes are used in the plan. The drive crosses the first lake, offering a graded elective carry. The extremely long player may reach far enough to take a full "soak" with his brassy across the second lake to the green. (The photograph was taken from a point near the green looking back along this shot which would cross the water at a point over the two felled trees.) But ordinarily the hole will be a three-shotter, with the second along the second lake to open up the green to an accurate approach. It will be interesting to know that as a two-shotter the hole will call for about four hundred and sixty yards, which none other than the most courageous smiters will attempt, while the three-shot player will cover nearly a hun-

Golf Illustrated *(A. W. Tillinghast)*

THE "OLD SOAK" BEARS A VERY OBVIOUS NAME. MANY A MISS-TIMED SHOT WILL FIND A LIQUID GRAVE THERE.

dred yards more. The possibility of finding either of the two lakes is a further warrant for its name.

Certain it is that the water holes are popular. There is the mental hazard as the great factor, and the average golfer likes to court danger occasionally, provided the architect gives him a safer way around if desired, but probably they meet with so much favor because they generally are attractive to look upon, with a marked individuality. To be sure, there are so-called water holes which are little more than frog ponds, covered with slime and stagnant, where the larvae of the mosquito thrive. These represent faulty construction, and usually reveal outlets badly clogged with vegetation. It is not difficult to introduce the water hazard, and another article deals with them in detail. They are discussed now wholly as outstanding features which go so far to make the course beautiful. They offer a distinct change from the holes over meadowlands, which so frequently are monotonous and featureless, and entirely without reason—for there is absolutely no excuse for a featureless hole anywhere on any course. A round of golf should present eighteen inspirations—not necessarily thrills, for spectacular holes may be sadly overdone. Every hole may be constructed to provide charm without being obtrusive with it. When I speak of a hole being inspiring, it is not intended to infer that the visitor is to be subject to attacks of hysteria on every teeing ground as he casts his eye over the fairway to the green for the first time, and to be so overwhelmed with the outstanding features, both natural and manufactured, that he can not keep his eye on the ball. It must be remembered that the great majority of golfers are aiming to reduce their previous best performance by five strokes if possible, first, last and all the time, and if any one of them arrives at the home teeing ground with this possibility in reach, he is not caring two hoots whether he is driving off from nearby an ancient oak of majestic size and form or a dead sassafras. If his round ends happily it is one beautiful course. Such is human nature.

Photo by Lynn Shackelford *(A. W. Tillinghast)*

THE APPROPRIATELY NAMED "DUEL HOLE" AT SAN FRANCISCO GOLF CLUB HAS QUITE AN INDIVIDUALITY OF ITS OWN. TILLINGHAST EXPLAINS: "...IN THE YEAR 1859, THE LAST FORMAL DUEL IN THE UNITED STATES WAS FOUGHT, BETWEEN U.S. SENATOR DAVID C. BRODERICK, OF CALIFORNIA, AND SUPREME COURT JUDGE DAVID S. TERRY. BRODERICK WAS ADVERSE TO DUELING BUT RECOGNIZED THE NECESSITY OF ACCEPTING THE CHALLENGE AS A MAN OF HONOR, FEARING THAT HIS POLITICAL FRIENDS PARTICULARLY WOULD CHARGE HIM WITH COWARDICE IF HE DECLINED. HE WAS SHOT DEAD."

But in every human there lurks somewhere the admiration of the beautiful, and there are few, indeed, who are so callused that the emphasized features of a golf hole will not sink in somewhere and make him enjoy his round, even though it is subconscious. Let us suppose, for example, that there happens to be a fine old apple tree near a teeing ground, where sometimes players may have to wait. It is more than likely that the architect has so arranged the hole that the old tree is featured there, and a circular bench has been built around the tree.

Maybe someone, who has closed his desk in town and taken to the links for real recreation, sits there and as he waits the old tree suddenly seems friendly—and maybe he recalls just such a tree from which, years ago, a small boy filled his shirt with apples, all the while ready to cut and run if the farmer happened along. With that memory, no matter if the round runs into three figures, the afternoon's golf has been something more than a game after all.

The crack players demand real testing holes. This is entirely as it should be, but they too, will find a new sting to their shots if the surroundings make them feel that they are playing no common, low-down hole. No hole need be formal and ugly to be a true test of playing ability. The National Links offers one of the hardest tests of the game in the world, and the course is beautiful and inspiring. It represents the exact opposite of the inland course, and its treatment is a monument to its creator.

During the past fifteen years the writer has come in contact with thousands who have their own ideas concerning courses. During the last five years these lay ideas were advanced in great numbers and along different lines than formerly. In every section of the country the demand is for sound courses, but above all they want the beautiful. To be frank, half the time the builders of new courses have no ideas concerning the character of the holes or their distribution, and without hesitation put this squarely up to the architect, trusting to his reputation to produce something which will give them pleasure to play, and nine times in ten there is the dominating thought of the beauties of the course. The study of these desires seems to be the real secret of modern course building, and one cannot conceive any hole which is not featured along well-defined lines which every hole must suggest naturally. In planning eighteen holes there are thousands of combinations, each offering a mute appeal for recognition. It is necessary, of course, to decide on the collection which will work out economically and satisfactorily from many angles. But this is sure: every hole must have individuality and be sound. Often it is necessary to get from one section to another over ground which is not suited to the easiest construction, but that troublesome hole must be made to stand right up in meeting with the others, and if it has not got anything about it that might make it respectable, it has got to have quality knocked into it until it can hold its head up in polite society.

Many committees are returning to the old custom of naming the holes of their courses. To me this was always pleasing

Photo by Lynn Shackelford *(A. W. Tillinghast)*

ANOTHER OF TILLINGHAST'S FAVORITE HOLES, THE TENTH AT WINGED FOOT WEST.

and when the practice disappeared generally, I was very loath to see it pass. Now there is a revival. Many courses are changed from time to time. Sometimes the committee deems it wise to change the playing order. When this is done, immediately the holes are difficult to remember when discussing them, apart from the links.

The most famous holes on British courses were referred to by names: The Redan at North Berwick, for example; the Station Master's Garden at St. Andrews. Everywhere they were known by these names, and they still are. It is not because the custom is followed in Great Britain that I advocate it, but because it is sensible. The naming of a good hole certainly adds to its distinction. It gives it an individuality.

~

Editor's Note
Robert Hunter and Hazards

There are several components of modern golf architecture that make it a complex profession and certainly, an inexact science. However, one quality of our modern courses that requires minimal thought and planning, yet determines the reputation of any new course, are its hazards and their placement. Over and over again in modern architecture, we see hazards placed merely for aesthetic reasons or simply to punish a bad shot that is already in serious trouble even if it were not in the hazard.

In "The Purpose of Hazards," Robert Hunter defines why we need hazards and how they should be placed throughout a golf course to create an exciting test for all levels of play. Hunter's friend, Alister MacKenzie, described the placing of hazards quite well himself: "It is an interesting fact that few hazards are of any interest which are out of what is known to medical men as the direct field of vision. This does not extend much further than ten to twenty yards on either side of the direct line to the hole. Hazards placed outside these limits are usually of little interest, and are simply a source of irritation. Hazards should be placed with an object in mind, and not one should be made which has not some influence on the line of play to the hole."

G.S.

~

The Purpose of Hazards

by Robert Hunter
The Fairway
March 1922

Without well-moulded greens with true surfaces no golf can be pleasurable, and without plenty of well-placed hazards no golf can satisfy the sporting instinct. Bunkers make dramatic golf. They provide the thrills and feed man's appetite for adventure. They are, moreover, the decisive influence in the making of golfers. They fashion the shots of the youth. Let the greens be well guarded, and the youth will learn to pitch and stop. With undulations before him, he will become adept at placing his shots. Build plenty of hazards on the borders of the fairways and he will learn to keep down the middle, and give him a few heroic carries to make and the result will be all that can be desired. In the old days one could often tell whence a golfer came by the shots he had. The St. Andrews man could rarely pitch well but his run-ups were marvelous to behold. He was often also a wild hitter because that paid best at St. Andrews, where some of the worst bunkers are in the middle of the course. At Sandwich I noticed that even the older habitue had a fine carry, that being an essential there. And if a first-rate course will produce fine golfers among the youth, it will also vastly improve the golf of the older members. Older men rarely improve their game when they habitually play on broad, hazardless fairways with nothing to do when they are hitting badly.

Where every shot is "as good as a better" there is no need to improvement, and, generally speaking, none is made. Almost invariably these older men are annoyed when there is talk of improving "the old course," and almost invariably they are delighted after they have played for a while on the new product.

Yet one must sympathize with older men and indifferent players, who have little time to improve their game and wish to enjoy their limited leisure in some sport not too exacting. When they have done their best they resent finding their ball again and again in some hideous chasm. Of course this can only happen on a badly planned course. The first-rate architects feel it to be a duty to make the path of the weaker players comparatively easy while presenting to the scratch man a route to the hole that is fraught with difficulty. It may seem to some that this is impossible, but the thing has been done again and again. More than any other attainment of the best modern architects, this achievement fills the student of this art with unbounded admiration. Hazards bordering the fairway at say from 165 to 210 yards from the tee, traps en echelon and diagonal bunkers are not as likely to bother the short hitter as the man who is going out for pars. On a hole of 400 yards the short hitter must take three shots whether or not there are traps on the way. With well-placed hazards, he must be more accurate but that is all that is required of him while the long hitter seeking his par must flirt with danger all the way and if he slips he may even lose the hole to his weaker opponent.

There are two holes at St. Andrews which illustrate what is meant. They are both short holes, and short holes are the most difficult of all to make playable for all classes of golfers and yet remain a test for the champion. The eighth is a hole of 140 yards which can be played equally well with a slice, a pull or a pitch and run, but whatever way one chooses to play the hole it must be a perfect shot of its kind. The eleventh at St. Andrews is even more remarkable. It can be played with a putter and yet one could understand a great champion facing this hole in a critical round with the prayer, "O Lord, be merciful!"

The Redan at North Berwick is another such hole. It is often said to be the best one-shot hole in the realm of golf. It has been copied again and again by enterprising architects, and several replicas are now to be found in this country. It is 200 yards in length and an easy enough 4 for the short accurate hitter, but the man who plays for its par must execute perfectly one of three possible shots. With wind ahead he must play a high slice with his driver, a dead straight spoon shot or a low-flying ball with a sharp pull at the finish. Such holes as these

Ralph Miller Golf Library *(MacKenzie and Hunter)*

ALISTER MACKENZIE AND ROBERT HUNTER'S PAR-3 THIRD HOLE AT CYPRESS POINT GOLF CLUB BEFORE OPENING.

make one hesitate to be dogmatic on the question of placing of bunkers. There are scores of hazards on the best seaside courses in exactly those places where even the most foolhardy American architect would never venture to place one, and yet these very hazards, which often punish well-played shots, are the features which render the play there indescribably fascinating. Moreover, one is astonished to see what low scores short accurate hitters often return in competitions.

In placing hazards let there always be clearly in mind what one desires to accomplish. Unless there is some well-defined purpose in mind, hazards may often become merely a source of irritation. If it is desired to punish the bad shots, ask one's self, whose bad shots? It is better not to punish bad shots on certain holes which are often as good as the best. How often one sees at unguarded greens a half-topped mashie run dead to the hole while a well-played pitch effects nothing. How often on a down grade a topped drive will run farther than a well-hit carrying ball. How often on holes of medium length a wild hook or vicious slice costs the offender nothing. Such bad shots should be punished, and in most cases it is not a difficult thing to do. And here the purpose is quite distinct, but we should not forget that such hazards rarely add interest to the play, and this it seems to me should be the main consideration. There is nothing more enjoyable in life, whether at work or at play, than to set for one's self some ideal and by one's own effort to achieve it. And this is particularly true of golf. Where does one hear so much talk about any achievement in life as in a golf club after the day's play is over? "I did the fifth hole in 3 today." "I carried that far bunker on the twelfth!" "You ought to have seen my pitch to the sixth over that new trap!" and so on. Rather dreadful, but we all have to hear it. And without these thrills, golf would lose its interest for most of us.

Well-placed traps provide the opportunity to achieve something unusual and, if golfers kept that thought in mind, even when they find themselves bunkered, they would play their shots with a different spirit. Accurate hitting, that is to say, having your club meet the ball in a definite manner, is an essential in every good shot. The way the club should meet the ball varies. In some shots the face of the club should be rising, in others descending and in still others it should be drawn slightly across the ball. Occasionally the ball should be taken clean; at other times the club should bite into the turf just as it meets the ball. The best players are those who can most accurately place their club on the ball in the manner required for the particular shot desired. Getting out of trouble is easier for such players because accurate hitting is here usually a *sine qua non.*

Anyone wishing to improve the accuracy of his hitting could do nothing better than to spend an hour or so with different clubs playing shots out of the sand. You can there easily determine in just what manner your club is meeting the ball. Such practice is tiring, but without it no youth will become a champion and few older men improved golfers. Moreover, most bunker shots will become for you quite as easy as some shots from the fairway, and to find yourself in trouble will not seem to you a tragedy but an opportunity to exhibit your skill.

~

Editor's Note
George Thomas and One-Shotters

Few architects are more qualified than George C. Thomas Jr. to comment on the "lure, intrigue and importance of the one-shotter." A wealthy Philadelphian who emigrated to Southern California in 1920, Thomas grew up "in golfing knowledge" with some of the finest par-3s in existence at Pine Valley and Merion.

It wasn't until he moved West that Thomas really practiced what he preached, building some of the most memorable one-shotters in golf. The sixth at Riviera, with a tiny bunker in the middle of the green, is certainly his most famous. But his best work may have been a series of long, "modified Redans" at the Los Angeles Thomas Triumvirate: Bel-Air, Riviera, and Los Angeles Country Club's North Course. Each modified Redan was built with the principles of the North Berwick original in mind. However, Thomas built his Redans to be much longer, usually requiring a driver. (He became quite defensive about the length of these holes after the fourth at Riviera was criticized by touring pros in the early days. Some years later Ben Hogan called Riviera's fourth "the greatest par-3 hole in America.")

A rosarian at heart, George Thomas was a man of many tastes. His passion for the "Queen of Flowers" continued throughout his life, while other hobbies came and went. He was a dedicated World War I pilot, crashing three times and doling out part of his sizable family fortune to fund his squadron's mission. In California he devoted most of his early days to golf architecture before spending his final years enamored with deep sea fishing. Thomas authored two classic books on roses, another on deep sea fishing, and in 1927 published what has become a favorite in golf literature: *Golf Architecture in America, Its Strategy and Construction.*

Within *Golf Architecture in America* Thomas covers a variety of subjects, from strategy ("the soul of the game") to intelligent construction practices. Captain Thomas also writes of one-shotters and their importance, though not in the detail he does for the following article.

"The Theory and Architecture of the One-Shot Hole" appeared in the January 1932 issue of *Game and Gossip Magazine*, an obscure West Coast society magazine for the wealthy and beautiful. This was to be the first of three articles for *Game and Gossip*, the other two, naturally, on three-shotters and two-shotters. But Thomas suffered a fatal heart attack a month after the first essay was published. In what turned out to be his final article, Thomas displays his wit along with many sound ideas about par-3s and their importance in the scheme of the design. He also saves some fascinating and somewhat cynical remarks for the USGA on their then ever-changing rules for the design and weight of the golf ball.

G.S.

~

The Theory and Architecture of the One-Shot Hole

by George C. Thomas, Jr.
Game and Gossip Magazine
January 1932

Thoroughly to enjoy golf, one should understand and appreciate something of the theory and strategy of the course. It was not built hit or miss, but constructed from principles constructed as axioms after years of trial, as suited to each particular problem.

The par-3 or one-shot is not only necessary for diversity and concentrated interest in the actual round of play, but also most convenient and practicable for using odd pieces of terrain left over from longer holes, or for linking other two and three-shot units.

Perhaps it is easier to construct a satisfactory one-shotter than to design and build longer holes, and yet there are factors in the development of the former which are distinct and unique. First of all, one realizes that the stroke to the green of a par-3 is from nearly constant points as designated by a fixed tee or tees, whereas, on two-shotters and three-shotters after drives and seconds, the approach to the flag is from varied angles and distances determined by many types of first and later shots.

This prearranged position for play to the cup enables the architect to demand more exactness in the drive to a one-shot green and usually develops much more interest in the initial effort on such a hole. The climax depends on the tee shot; there is no graduation of events. The designer may specify the length and character of stroke; he may construct his green so that a pitch is required or a running ball insisted upon. He may use more than one tee, and by varying the lengths and angles of the ball's flight, prepare his green for one particular kind of shot from one tee, and another type from other tees.

These underlying advantages in the basic principles of the one-shotter may be carried out by size, shape, and contour of green, as well as by artificial penalties, although as in longer holes, natural troubles are more to be desired than manufactured ones. Nevertheless, existing hazards are utilized with less fear of complications, because of the ability to plan the start. No matter what dangers are supplied, a really good par-3 example generally should have at least two tees, so that players of all kinds will be given a test commensurate with their ability.

The old adage of golf architecture, "the shorter the shot, the smaller the green," has been discarded as an accepted theory, on account of increased traffic on courses. We must now supply all greens with sufficient adaptable surface frequently to change the cup. The same crowded conditions necessitate a green without too many severe rolls or undulations, for the reason that steep slopes are not practicable to pin placements.

In addition, the designer must consider the ever-changing golf ball—aforetime, small and heavy and quite satisfactory, its evolution was a constant one along lines of increasing distance and better control in the air and on the ground.

Recently the U.S.G.A. forced first a lighter and larger sphere upon a long-suffering golf world, and this change gave less distance, poorer control aloft, and a more difficult ball to

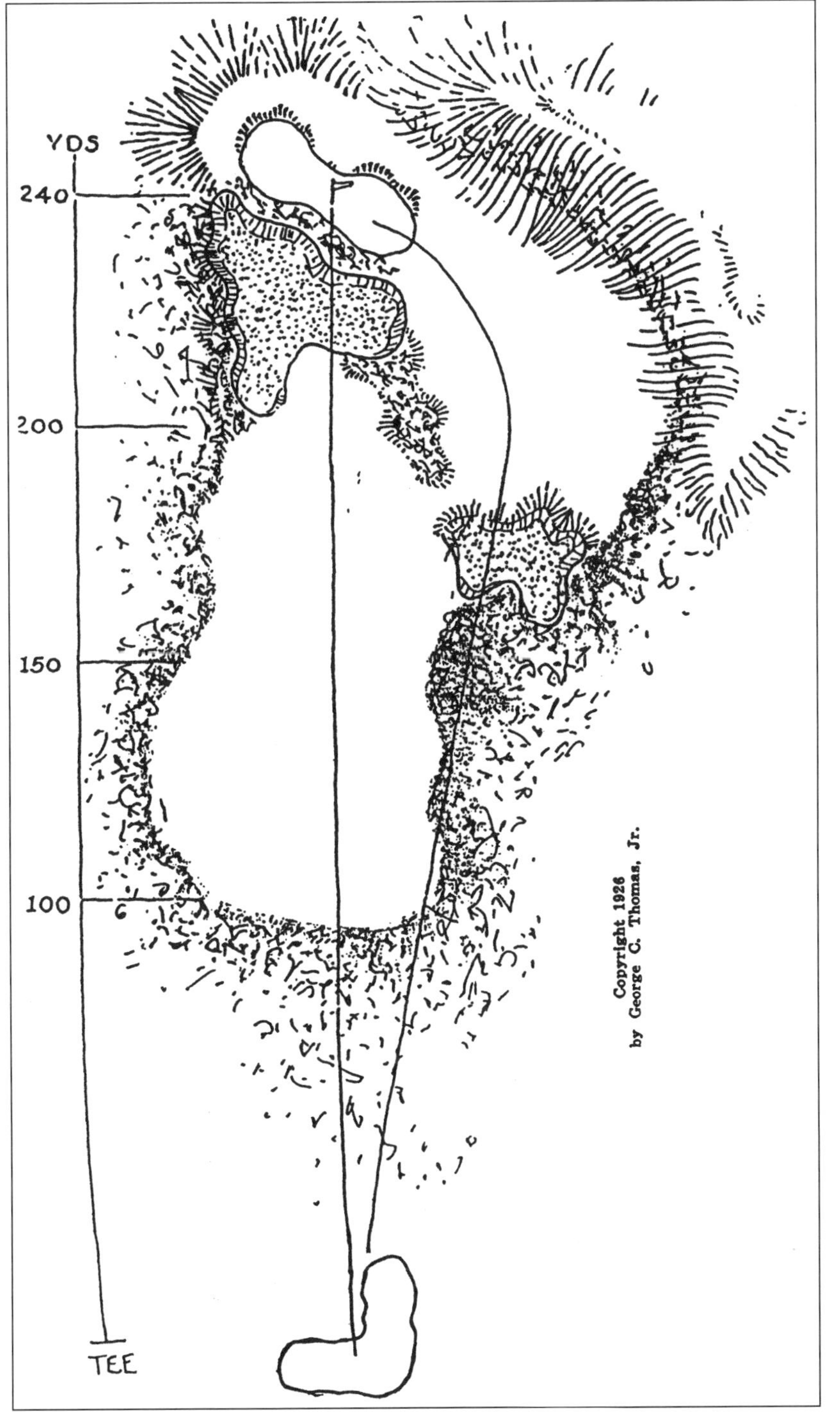

Mercury Magazine (*George C. Thomas Jr.*)

SKETCH BY GEORGE THOMAS OF HIS "MODIFIED-REDAN" PAR-3 FOURTH, RIVIERA COUNTRY CLUB.

Ralph W. Miller Golf Library *(Thomas and Bell)*

THOMAS'S MOST FAMOUS ONE-SHOTTER, THE SIXTH AT RIVIERA.
NOTE THE BUNKER IN THE MIDDLE OF THE GREEN.

putt. Next we find another new ball, of the same size as the one just discarded, but of heavier weight. This latest official pronouncement, while apparently superior in some measure, must be played before criticized, although it is hard for the average golfer, let alone architect, to understand why a difficult game has been made more exacting with the discarding of the small, heavy ball, satisfactory to most players, particularly as Britain has not followed the U.S.G.A. lead.

These changes of golf balls make the problem of the constructor more confused than ever, because he must endeavor to prepare his entire course for a variable standard, and must provide, for the exasperating problem, a green which later will take

USGA *(Crump and Colt)*

THE PAR-3 THIRD AT PINE VALLEY GOLF CLUB, CIRCA 1940.

care of any oval, balloon, or cannon-ball upon which the governing body may insist.

However, other fundamentals of construction regulated by ground conditions and by atmosphere and weather fortunately remain as heretofore. The speed of different soils affects the shot to all greens and a varying or nearly constant wind direction is as important as in the past. Wet and dry climatic changes must not be overlooked.

- The selection of 3 pars sometimes is supposed to be limited to four examples on eighteen holes—two on each nine. Yet the other units and their character and distance must determine the number, yardage and kind of one-shotters.

On a course with more than two 5 pars, or where there are more than four long and difficult two-shotters, it is advisable to consider the use of five one-shot greens. Conversely, on courses with more than four short two-shotters, or with only one 5 par, it is wise to restrict the use of one-shotters to three holes. For reasons of diversification, short 3 par holes are best on a course with many long two-shotters, and long 3 pars called for where there are many short 4 pars.

If the links are well-balanced with fine 5 pars and a proper number of good long and short two-shotters, it will be possible and very satisfactory to vary the kind of 3 pars on such a high-class course, providing many types of endeavor. Five splendid one-shot greens are not too many. Imagine the distinction of portraying five nearly perfect 3 pars. Visualize an exacting mashie niblick pitch as one, an attractive run-up for a short-iron giving a second, a fine, medium iron demanding a third, a long iron or a spoon as a fourth, and a full drive for a fifth. Surely such variation is well worthwhile.

- One-shotters, to enhance their own interest and the charm of all other holes, must give a radical change in length and class of shot to the holes preceding and following. What is sadder than a short two-shotter, next, a one-shot niblick and following the latter another two-shotter lacking in distance, thereby continuing the same or nearly the same short approach? One-shotters should seldom follow one another, and it is inadvisable to have them among the first three holes because they congest the start of a round, and they should not be used as finishing units, particularly short 3 pars.
- The up-to-date course must contain fine examples of 3 pars. Such stand out in one's mind with distinctness—per-

> haps with more emphasis than they deserve. Oftimes an entire test is made prominent by a noted one-shot hole, and it has happened that an otherwise acceptable layout has been severely criticized for two or even a single poor 3 par hole.

Who shall say which par affords the most superlative play? No one will deny the lure, intrigue, and importance of the one-shotter.

~

Editor's Note
Macdonald, Whigham and the Redan

If a contemporary golf architect took the concept of the Redan and built a replica of the famed par-3 on each of his courses, that architect would almost certainly get blasted by the today's golf media. However, over seventy years since Charles Blair Macdonald and his associate Seth Raynor went around the country building courses with a prescribed group of holes on each layout, the concept has become a timeless signature of their work. Aficionados of Macdonald and Raynor love to compare the Redan, or the Cape, from one of their creations to another.

Perhaps a modern day architect would have trouble carrying off this concept because we rarely see courses constructed with the care and subtlety that Macdonald and Raynor put into their work. It should be noted that even though some of their Redans are quite similar, the real interest for aficionados lies in the differing terrain used to construct the Redans. In the following article, Macdonald and his son-in-law H.J. Whigham explain exactly what the Redan is, and why it is unparalleled.

H.J. Whigham wrote a series of articles for *Golf Illustrated* with Macdonald upon the opening of The National Golf Links. Each piece focused on one of the holes which Macdonald was designing based on principles of great holes he had seen in Scotland. Besides the Redan article, Macdonald and Whigham wrote about the "Cape," "Alps," and "Sahara" holes at The National.

Whigham wrote four books on various subjects and served as Editor of *Country Life Magazine* for 25 years. He was one of America's first prolific players, winning the U.S. Amateur in 1896 and 1897. In 1907 Whigham married Macdonald's daughter Francis, and over the following years wrote several articles on architecture, most of which made glowing references to the work of, you guessed it, Charles Blair Macdonald!

G.S.

~

Redan Hole at The National Golf Links

by C.B. Macdonald and H.J. Whigham
Golf Illustrated
July 1914

Take a narrow tableland, tilt it a little from right to left, dig a deep bunker on the front side, approach it diagonally, and you have the Redan. At North Berwick, of course, all these things were done in the beginning by nature. The only original thing that the greenkeeper did was to place the tee so that the shot had to played cornerwise, so to speak, instead of directly down the tableland. And when you come to think of it that is the secret of most of the great holes all over the world. They all have some kind of a twist.

Said the North Berwick caddie to Mr. Macdonald when he was on the quest for ideal holes for the coming National Links. "Here's the hole that makes a man think." Then he took a handful of grass and threw it in the air to see exactly in what direction the light breeze was blowing. For there are more ways of playing the Redan than any other short hole in existence. The force and direction of the wind not only determines the club to be chosen and the strength to be used, but also the direction and character of the stroke. The tableland is long and narrow, sloping from right to left; there is a deep bunker in front and a smaller bunker at the back. It would be almost impossible to drop the ball on the green near the flag and keep it there if the green were not banked a little from the center of the tee. With a head wind or one coming a little from the left a wooden club may be used and the shot played straight at the flag, for then the ball will drop dead on the green. But it is a long carry over the deep bunker in the face of the green, and because the direction is diagonal the carry gets longer and longer to the left, so that the least bit of pull will put the ball into the bunker. With no wind at all the same kind of shot can be played with a mid-iron, but it must be a high shot that will drop very dead, the most difficult stroke in golf. With any wind behind, the direct attack becomes almost impossible, and then the player must aim for the right-hand end of the green where he does not have to carry the deep bunker in the face. The ball landing on the high end of the tableland will break to the left, and will be kept going more to the left by the fact that the green is banked like a circular bicycle track, and so a shot played twenty yards or more to the right of the hole may end up within a foot of the flag. But it has to be played just right. The least bit of pull will take it into the bunker in front of the green, and the least slice will prevent it getting the break to the left and will carry it into the bunker beyond the green. With a strong wind behind the hole it is still more difficult, for it must then be played with a very lofted club, or else with a running shot which must carry the large bunker to the right, which as a rule hardly enters into one's calculations, and get pulled up on the side of the tableland. Either shot admits of all kinds of error.

The principle of the Redan can be used wherever a long narrow tableland can be found or made. Curiously enough the Redan existed at the National long before the links was thought of. It is a perfectly natural hole. The essential part, the tilted tableland was almost exactly like the North Berwick original. All that had to be done was to dig the bunker in the face, and place the tee properly. The National Redan is rather more difficult than the North Berwick hole, because the bunker at the back of the green is much deeper and more severe. Some people think the hole is too difficult altogether. But anyone who gets a legitimate three there, especially in a medal round, is sure to say that it is the finest short hole in the world. There is no compromise about it. Whichever of the various methods of attack is chosen, the stroke must be bold, cleanly hit and deadly accurate. At the ordinary hole of 180 yards it is a very bad shot that does not stay on the green. At the Redan it takes an exceedingly good shot to stay anywhere on the green; and to get a putt for a two is something to brag about for a week.

There are several Redans to be found nowadays on American courses. There is a simplified Redan at Piping Rock, a reversed Redan at Merion Cricket Club (the green being approached from the left-hand end of the tableland), and another reversed Redan at Sleepy Hollow where the tee instead of being about level with the green is much higher. A beautiful short hole with the Redan principle will be found on the new Philadelphia course at Pine Valley. Here also the tee is higher than the hole, so that the player overlooks the tableland. The principle can be used with an infinite number of variations on any course. In reality there are only about four or five kinds of good holes in golf. The local scenery supplies the variety. Here is one of the four or five perfect kinds. The principle of the Redan cannot be improved upon for a hole of 180 yards.

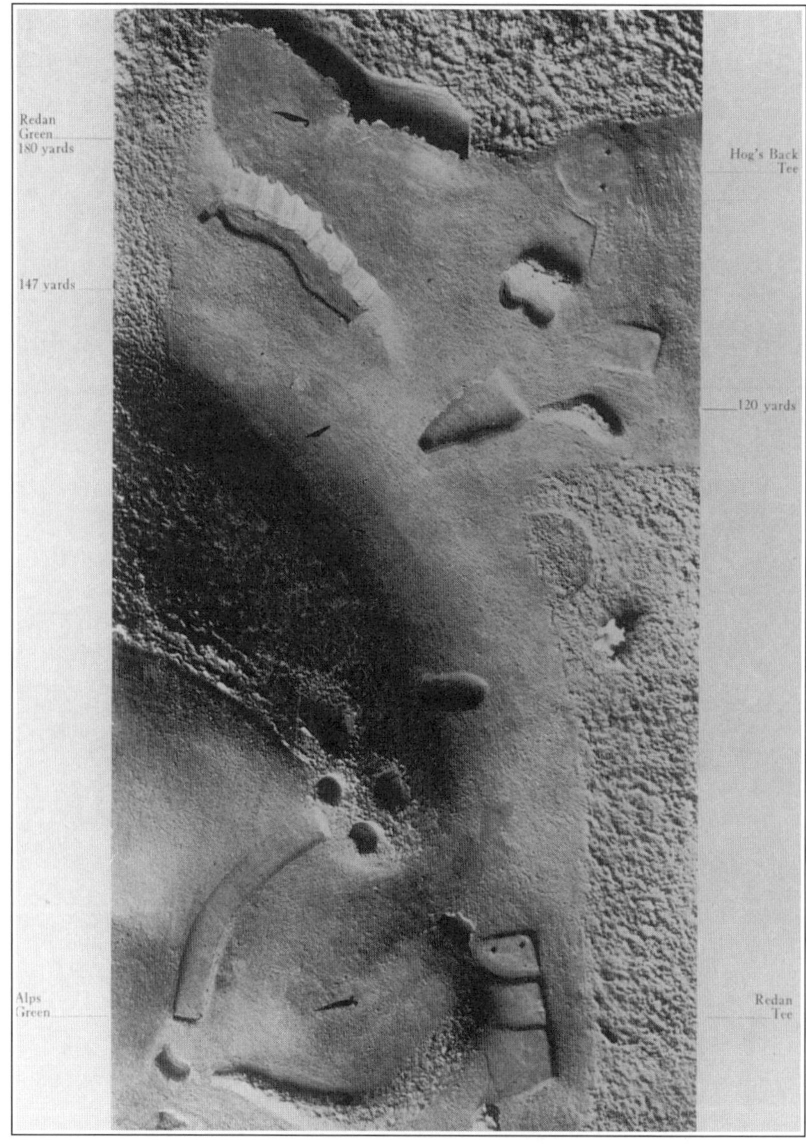

Golf Illustrated *(Macdonald and Raynor)*

THE REDAN HOLE, 180 YARDS, NATIONAL GOLF LINKS. SURVEYED AND MODELLED BY OSCAR SMITH, JR., OF F.S. TAINTER AND COMPANY.

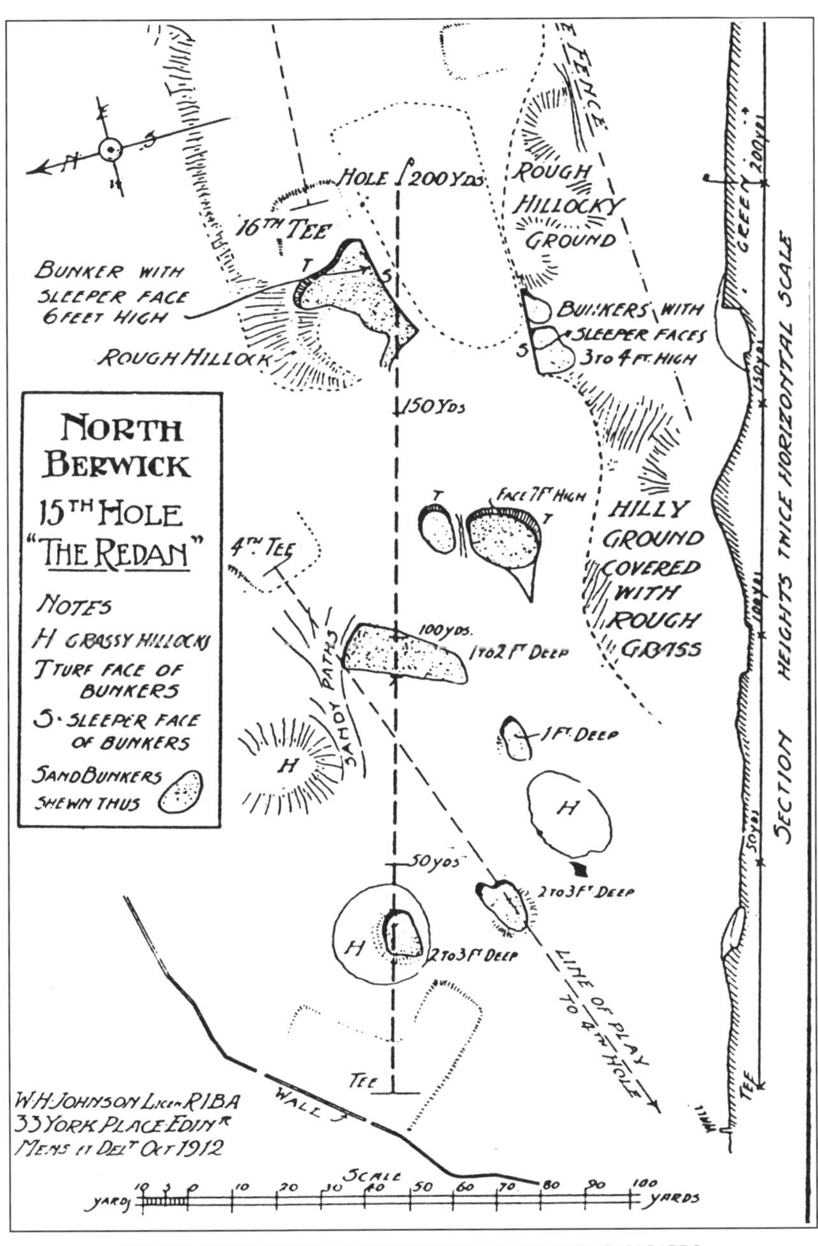

SKETCH OF THE ORIGINAL REDAN FROM ALEC BAUER'S *HAZARDS*.

~

Editor's Note
MacKenzie and Water Hazards

"Water Holes Should Tempt, Not Torture," was the first of Alister MacKenzie's posthumously published articles to appear, showing up in Herb Graffis's sister publication to *Golfdom*, named *Golfing Magazine*. Those familiar with MacKenzie's epic book, *The Spirit of St. Andrews*, will recognize portions of "Water Holes" from the doctor's recently discovered manuscript.

What the reader finds in any MacKenzie article is that no matter what the subject, he usually wrote with the same purpose: to make the game better and to improve the enjoyment for the average player. In his obituary of Alister MacKenzie, *Golfing* publisher Herb Graffis succinctly summarizes why MacKenzie may have been the greatest of all architects: "I had the privilege of frequent contact with him and shall always remember how often he used that word "pleasurable" as the test of golf architecture . . . One phrase that Mac told me, I've thought was a gem of a description of good architecture: 'Make it look hard and play easy if the player uses his brains.'"

G.S.

~

Water Holes Should Tempt, Not Torture

by Dr. Alister MacKenzie
Golfing Magazine
January 1934

Being a Scotsman, I am naturally opposed to undiluted water. The admixture of water with both highballs and hazards is an art depending to a great extent on the right time and the right place.

My Scotch blood comes to the fore again in prejudicing me against any hazards which create the expense, annoyance and irritation of losing balls or even searching for them. Nevertheless, there are occasions when water hazards have their value, and if we ever return to the floater ball this value would be increased many fold.

The attitude of golfers and golf committees are amazingly inconsistent regarding water hazards. On two occasions recently when designing a course I have been requested to avoid most beautiful lakes and yet on other occasions I have been asked to make a lake at enormous expense when there was not one existing, and when far more spectacular hazards could be made in other ways at a tenth of the cost. At other times, in advising the improvements of a course, I have come across committees whose sole idea consists of putting a dirty little muddy pond somewhere on the course.

Twenty years ago my brother played with me for the first time at Alwoodly, a course we were very proud of and thought, and still think, the best inland course in Britain. My brother topped three balls into the one and only pond on the course. When he returned to the clubhouse and was asked his opinion of the course he replied, and incidentally it was the only comment he made, "You've got too many ruddy ponds about."

The Lindbergh Thrill

The desirability or otherwise of having water hazards depends largely on their spectacular character and beauty. The amazing thrill of driving successfully over the ocean at the 16th hole at Cypress Point more than compensates for the loss of a dozen balls. Even absolute dubs succumb to this thrill.

The Spirit of St. Andrews *(MacKenzie and Hunter)*

DR. MACKENZIE POSES ON A WATER HOLE THAT CERTAINLY TEMPTS, AND OCCASIONALLY TORTURES.

Early one morning I was taking photographs at Cypress Point and met a man and his wife playing the ocean holes. They were absolute dubs; I doubt if they could break 150 on any course. I remarked that they were up early and they said, "Oh, we did not start at the first tee; we are just playing the ocean holes, 15th, 16th, 17th and 18th, four times over to make up a round."

If a spectacular water hazard occurs naturally like the ocean at Cypress Point I am strongly in favor of utilizing it to the fullest extent, but a water hazard created artificially is rarely worth while unless it can be done cheaply and serves an additional purpose, such as a reservoir for irrigation water. Even so, an artificial lake of this kind should have a clear bottom so that balls can be recovered, and it is also essential that it should be made so artistically and beautifully that it cannot be distinguished from a natural lake. There is no thrill in driving over an ugly hazard.

I remember many years ago seeing a peppery Major at Strensall in Yorkshire, England, top three balls into an extremely muddy pond. The ugliness of the hazard and his bad play irritated him so much that he threw his club after his ball, then he threw his whole bag in and when his small caddie began to laugh he chucked him in too!

For more than twenty years I have advocated that every hole on a golf course should have an alternative route for even the weakest of players. If this is not so, how can we expect new recruits to the game? The average beginner cannot lift his ball off the ground and how much more so is this the case when he knows that failure to do so will result in his losing his ball in a fearsome-looking water hazard!

Another Way Around

It is of paramount importance, therefore, that there should always be a way round for the novice in order that he may, with the loss of one or two strokes, eventually reach the green.

There are, of course, natural hazards such as rivers, which it is sometimes impossible to negotiate in this way. In cases of this kind it is often desirable to make a local rule to minimize their disadvantages. There was a club I belonged to more than thirty years ago, Ilkley in England where Tom Vardon was professional. A river ran through the grounds several times in the course of a round. The course was not popular. Members lost so many balls in the water that the committee was forced to make a local rule to the effect that a ball could be dropped on the opposite bank of the river, if possible no nearer the hole, for the loss of a stroke. At the ocean hole, the 16th at Cypress Point, we have a similar local rule and this in spite of the fact that it is possible to play round the ocean.

One time while traveling East I met a man, affectionately known as Billy Humphries, and he said to me, "What sort of a hole do you think your 16th is at Cypress Point?"

I asked him what he had on his mind and he replied, "Well I do not consider any hole is 'golf ' which can be played with a putter."

"On the contrary," I said, "I do not consider any hole ideal that cannot be played with a putter. But what is your trouble?"

He said, "I was playing the 16th with Herbert Flieschaker for $200. (Flieschaker is a very short driver but a man who uses his head.) I put two shots into the ocean. Then Herbert takes his putter, reaches the green in four (the 16th is a one-shot hole), holes a long putt and gets my two hundred dollars!"

The Far Famed Swilken

Perhaps the most famous of all water hazards is the "Swilken Burn," at the first hole on the Old Course at St. Andrews, Scotland. It is gross flattery to call it a burn; in reality it is a muddy sewer, but owing to the peculiar formation of the loop, it makes an ideal first hole.

It is 360 yards long and there are almost two hundred yards of wide open fairway to drive onto. Yet it is intensely interesting because every player takes into consideration the strength and direction of the wind and the position of the flag on the green before arriving at a decision whether to place his tee shot right, left or down the center so as to make his second shot an easier one.

Ralph W. Miller Golf Library

THE SWILKEN BURN AT ST. ANDREWS DURING THE OPEN CHAMPIONSHIP.

It was in connection not with Swilken Burn but a somewhat similar hazard on another Scottish course that a visitor one day asked what the members thought of the burn as a hazard. He was told that the attitude of a retired army officer summed up the general attitude of the members.

"What is that?" asked the visitor.

"Well," was the reply, "when the Major gets over it, he says to his caddie, 'Well ower the bonnie wee burn, ma laddie,' but when he gets into it he says, 'Pick ma ball out of that damned sewer.'"

In conclusion it should be emphasized that the more spectacular and beautiful a water hazard, the greater is the thrill of successfully negotiating it. A water hazard should, if possible, have a clear bottom so that balls may be recovered, an alternative route or routes should be provided, and above all the player who takes the biggest risk should have the greatest reward.

~

Editor's Note
Tillinghast and Length

The more I think on it, the more it's apparent that Tillinghast would have been a colossus today. The moderns would have been plowed under by a competitor who would not have hesitated to successfully bribe the Golf Digest selection panel, who could write complete English sentences, and who possessed a sense of irony.

—Frank Hannigan

In "The Fetish of Length," Tillinghast spoke out on a dilemma that has plagued golf since its inception in America. We are a country fascinated by numbers, rankings, and concrete methods for judging art. Simply put, we love numbers and awards.

This mentality has somehow invaded modern golf architecture, with 7,000 yards becoming a fixed number that designates whether a course is of championship caliber or not. You have to wonder what Tillinghast would say to those developers today who demand that their new course exceed 7,000 yards for marketing purposes. However, Tillie was a businessman, and he might have just found a way to make it work while supplying the average man a playable golf course. "The Fetish of Length" lets you be the judge.

G.S.

~

For the Good of the Game—The Fetish of Length

by A.W. Tillinghast
Golf Illustrated
March 1935

We regard the present tendency to stretch golf courses out to greater lengths than ever before, as an unfortunate and mistaken policy. To make our courses generally more enjoyable to the great majority, we rather incline to the conviction that shorter holes and smaller greens would be much better. The average golfer, who cannot begin to get the prodigious lengths of the mighty ones, does like to encounter holes that are not beyond the range of two of his best efforts. When he is forced to face the necessity of covering four hundred and sixty yards to accomplish this under normal conditions, he can't quite make it with any two shots in his bag. Yet a hole of this length and longer is plain duck soup to the great players with but a few exceptions. Certainly such holes must be provided for occasions when the big fellows are competing, but for the day-in and day-out play of the modest ones, who yet delight in calling themselves "golfers," considerably less length should be offered.

Of course, this highly desirable situation may be provided by having very long teeing grounds, or even auxiliary ones, which will permit of the placement of the markers out toward

USGA *(Crump, Colt, Tillinghast)*

THE SECOND SHOT VIEW ON THE BRILLIANT PAR-4 THIRTEENTH AT PINE VALLEY - A LONG HOLE WHICH WORKS WELL BECAUSE IT AFFORDS SEVERAL OPTIONS TO THE AVERAGE AND BELOW-AVERAGE PLAYERS.

the fronts. Undoubtedly this is the solution. But when the shorter ranges are not considered, or not possible because the teeing areas are restricted and insignificant, then the situation is deplorable. However, after looking over a number of the most recently constructed courses, we come flatly back to the observation of our opening paragraph. Why, it is actually a fact that we have encountered the effort to produce "the longest hole in the world." The merit of any hole is not judged by its length but rather by its interest and its variety as elective play is apparent. It isn't *how far* but *how good*!

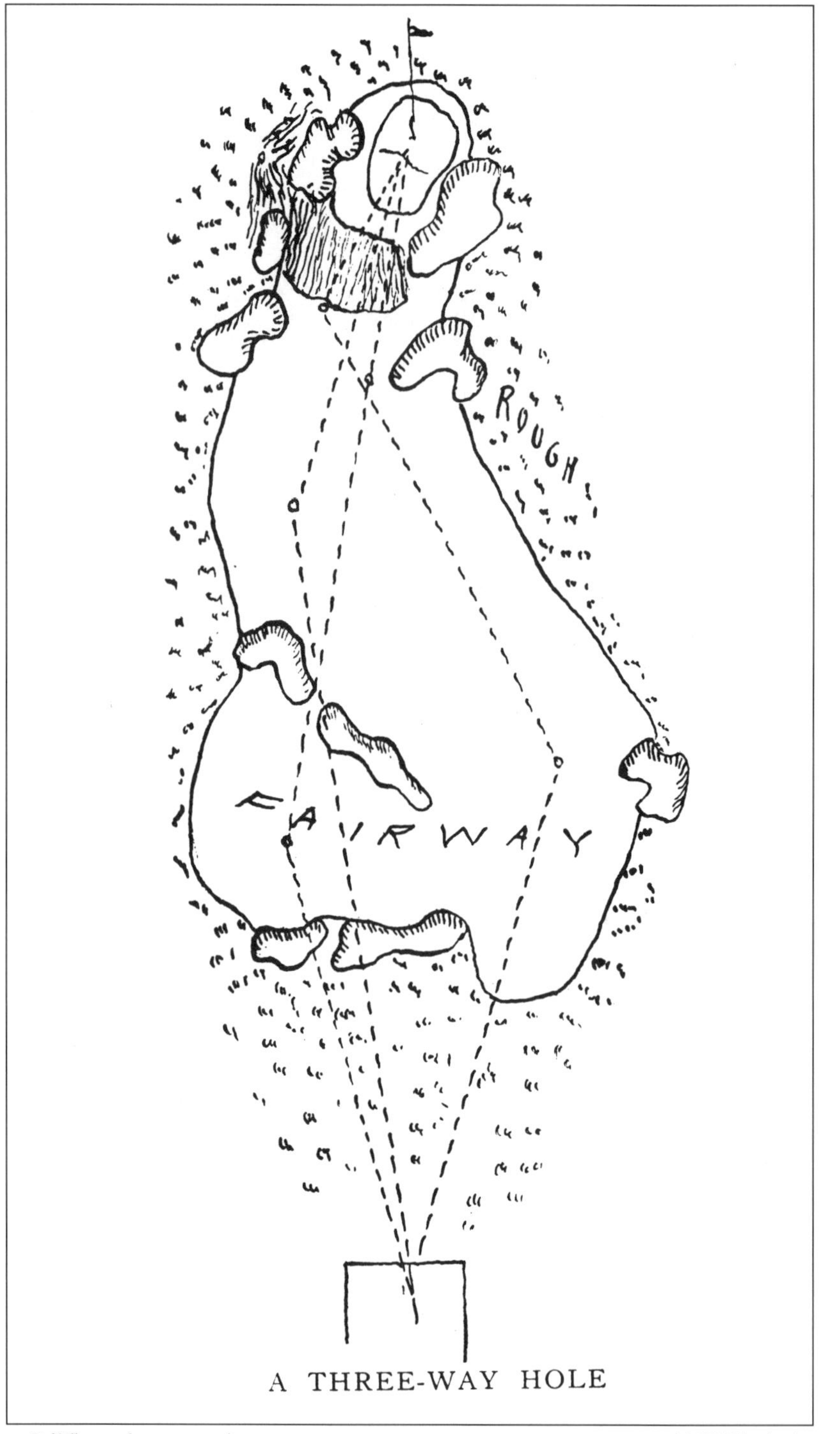

Golf Illustrated (*A.W. Tillinghast*)

IMAGINE HOW THE STRATEGY OF THIS HOLE WOULD BE ALTERED IF IT WERE LENGTHENED. SKETCH IS OF A PROPOSED "THREE-WAY" HOLE AT TILLINGHAST'S SAN FRANCISCO GOLF CLUB.

But the fetish of distance is worshipped entirely too often and there should be a quick end to it. Very recently, in California during one of the open tournaments, we heard a noted player asked his opinion of the course. "It's too damned long!" came the instant and candid reply—and this answer was made by one of the longest hitters in our land. And with this note of confidence from one for whom long holes have no terrors, we are for the present content to rest our case.

~

Editor's Note
Bernard Darwin and Difficulty

In "Who Wants the Course Made Harder?" Bernard Darwin makes the point that it is often the weaker players at a course or club who fear that their layout is being rendered defenseless. I can attest to his statements, as I have sat through endless Green Committee meetings when the most average of players will scream that the course is somehow being compromised by the cutting down of rough or the widening of fairways. Yet, this cry comes from those who usually can't break 80, 90, or even 100!

Darwin examines this peculiar mentality in golf, and it serves as a fitting follow-up to several of the articles in this book which underscore the importance of character, charm, and strategy in golf architecture over length, punishment, and anything that makes the game less interesting.

First, a few words on Darwin. The grandson of naturalist Charles Darwin, Bernard Darwin worked as a lawyer for many years before giving up his practice in 1908 to write about golf on a full-time basis. Darwin contributed to *Country Life Magazine* and the *Times* of London for over 45 years. Though golf was his primary passion, Darwin also wrote two biographies on nongolfers and his autobiography (*The World That Fred Made*).

The list of timeless golf books written by Darwin is far too long to list here, though classics like *The Golf Courses of the British Isles* and *Golf Between Two Wars* come to mind immediately. And don't be fooled by Darwin's modesty in the following article, or in his other writings; he was an outstanding player who reached the semifinals of the 1921 British Amateur, only to lose to the eventual winner, Willie Hunter.

What makes Darwin's writing so appealing and amusing? Not only did he document the history and courses of Great Britain in the manner that Herbert Warren Wind did in America, Darwin managed it with a sense of humor. Ben Crenshaw once described Darwin's style:

> He was the first golf writer to transcribe facts and figures into real journalism. He was unashamedly a lover of sports and games in general, and could never hide his deep affection for the game of golf. To me he appealed to the reader on the most individualistic terms. He TALKED to us, apologized to us, cried to us, bared his temper to us, and made us laugh with him, all in an attempt to reveal his deep love for golf to us. The world has been made better for it.

G.S.

~

Who Wants the Course Made Harder?

A Specific Case Showing that the High-Handicap Player Is Often the One

by Bernard Darwin

The American Golfer

February 1926

Which class of golfer is it that wants the links to be difficult? If that question were asked in a general assembly I fancy that the answer would be "Oh, the scratch players of course. All the other poor devils have to put up with it. I can't think why they don't make a revolution about it." It is the answer that I should have been inclined to give myself, but a day or two since I came across a piece of evidence that made me wonder if I was wrong.

I went to play at a well-known club near London of which I am a member, and, laid out on the table in the smoking room, I found two rival petitions addressed to the Committee and mutely appealing for my signature. The first of them set out that the signatories viewed with apprehension the recent cutting back of the heather as "being calculated to alter the character of the course." It was added in effect that if this cutting was done in order to make the carries less severe for lady players, this end could be better achieved by giving the ladies shorter tees.

The second document, a counter-blast to the first, did not

go into details but expressed confidence in the green committee and general approval of their doings. The interesting thing about the two documents was this. The signatories to the first were none of them very good players, and some were distinctly weak ones. There were several ladies among them of whom one was described a good player, but none of the others could be so by any stretch of chivalrous imagination. On the other hand, among those who signed the counter-blast there were no ladies but there was a male champion and several other players of repute.

This at first sight seemed to prove that it is the better players who like their golf made easier, but the matter is not really quite so simple. The cutting in question has not perceptibly widened the fairways of our course. The most it has done in that respect is to create at one or two holes a modified rough for the moderately crooked shot, a purgatory before the genuine hell of heather is reached. The main part of the cutting had been done in a straight line from tee to hole, so that the penalty for a topped shot is less heart breaking and the carries over solid heather are perhaps rather shorter than they used to be.

To the good player who drives a good long way and does so with fair regularity the changes really make no difference at all. He might play several rounds, if he were intent on his match, without observing that there was any change. Not so the weaker vessel to whom every tee shot is a separate adventure fraught with awful risks and corresponding possibilities of glory. He likes to be able to say, or at any rate to hug himself the reflection that he carried clear over the heather from the fourteenth tee against the wind. He is willing to run the risk and resents being robbed of the glory by this grandmotherly behavior

The American Golfer *(Crump and Colt)*

THE EIGHTH AT PINE VALLEY, SHOWING THE PENALTIES THAT AWAIT AN ERRANT SHOT, TYPICAL OF THAT GREAT COURSE. YET, EVEN THE HIGH-HANDICAP MEMBERS REVEL IN ITS DIFFICULTIES.

on the greens committee's part. Nor should this spirit be sneered at, for it is obviously a brave one.

The green committee's answer, I assume, will be twofold. First that all bad players that play on the course are not so brave as those signatories. Secondly, that the cutting was not done to make the golf easier, but to make it harder to lose balls. There is one thing in the game of golf which is entirely dreary and depressing, and that is looking for balls. Moreover it is depressing not only for those who look, but for those behind who have to wait while they are looking.

No doubt there are degrees of bravery among the weaker brethren; some are dogged wielders of the mashie and positively enjoy the feeling of endurance which comes of not giving in; others are softer and do not like the niblick play for its own sweet sake. The other day I played on the course in the park of one of the most famous of "the stately homes in England." There was one hole up a hill covered with trees and undergrowth. This was a comparatively long and formidable carry, but there was an easier way round. The noble owner of the course is not at all a good player but I was told that he always goes straight for this particular hole; not that he has ever surmounted the carry or ever hopes to do so, but simply that he believes in a frontal rather than a flanking attack, and that a steady ploughing through the woods is his idea of happiness.

I remember that when I visited that truly magnificent and truly terrifying course, Pine Valley, I remarked to one of my hosts that if the club had any members who were rather old or fat or unskillful, they must find it very hard work. He scouted the notion and declared that such members were as proud as a peacock and as happy as sand boys if they went around in 115 in place of their normal 120. That seems to show that in

Philadelphia, at any rate, the poorer golfers are not poor in the manly virtues.

I suppose the real fact is that the different classes of golfers do not differ in the courage with which they face difficulties. The ordinary carry from the tee scarcely exists for your fine long hitter who is also an accurate hitter. To him the tee-shot, though it never ceases to give physical pleasure, is yet a means to an end. To the inferior player it is an end in itself.

This difference is illustrated over here by two of our best known links, St. Andrews and Hoylake. To the player who is justified in reckoning his score by an average of fours both these courses are not only extremely interesting, but extremely searching tests of his skill. The moderate player, and still more the downright bad one, is often disappointed on a first visit and finds the golf dull. The reason is that on both courses, and especially at St. Andrews, there are few carries from the tee and a good deal of open country and so not much of the satisfaction which is to be got by hitting the ball a modest distance in the air.

I take it that the difficulty to which the humble golfer does object is that which comes from ever increasing length of holes. If ever there is a revolution of the golfing proletariat it will be on account of sheer length and not of fierce bunkers.

~

. . . the original charm of golf, its simplicity and naturalness, cannot be too strongly emphasized; and this was in a great measure lost when the demand for fresh courses grew, since it then became necessary to imitate what in the first instance had come into being spontaneously. There could never in the case of a repetition be quite the same originality or, for the matter of that, the same variety, qualities which all the old courses possessed in a supreme measure.

—H.N. Wethered and Tom Simpson

~

Part V

Contemporary Design

Our final section introduces us to issues in contemporary golf architecture. The essays included in Part V are written by several individuals who have demonstrated a genuine affection for golf architecture. Furthermore, they have demonstrated a love for the classics, whether it be through original design work, restoration, or in their writings. Tom Doak, one of the more interesting figures in modern architecture, gives an overview of the so-called "minimalist" movement and remarks on why it is so important to "Play It as It Lies." Part V then turns to some of the specific dilemmas in modern design, such as Pete Dye's fascinating explanation of "The Evolution of Green Speeds." Alice Dye illustrates why we need more thought put into the design of "forward" tees, and Gil Hanse clarifies why a golf course design must continue to evolve "in the field," an essay that will upset many architects who don't like to get their Bruno Maglis dirty.

Ron Forse writes on the sensitive subject of "To Tree or Not to Tree," followed by Bill Coore's "In Tribute to the Boys," a moving ode to the most important people in golf course architecture. I take a brief look at the irony in today's hazard maintenance, while Bobby Weed explains how courses can be better designed to avoid slow play in "Design for Speed." Ben Crenshaw comments on a disappearing breed in modern architecture: the short par-3. Finally, Bradley Klein concludes the book with some bold but necessary warnings about "When Architecture Becomes Big Business."

~

Editor's Note
Doak and Minimalism

Tom Doak has had what Ben Crenshaw calls "one of the finest educations of anyone in golf architecture." First, he studied at Cornell where he received the department's William F. Deer Award to study golf course architecture in the British Isles, during which time he visited 170 golf courses, including a two-month caddying stint on The Old Course at St. Andrews. After graduating, he apprenticed under Pete Dye at several of Mr. Dye's highest profile projects, including Long Cove Club on Hilton Head Island.

In 1989 he started Renaissance Golf Design and has since completed several highly regarded restorations, but it is Mr. Doak's original design work that has earned rave reviews from architecture aficionados. Relying on a style truly inspired by the classic designers from the "Golden Age" of architecture, Mr. Doak's design at Stonewall Golf Club in Philadelphia has quickly become one of that area's best courses with its sound strategy and sand-faced bunkering. His authentic links course at The Legends at Myrtle Beach is the most sophisticated design in the South Carolina resort town, while his strongest work to date may be his first design, the daily-fee High Pointe Golf Club in Doak's hometown of Traverse City, Michigan.

Tom Doak is a prolific writer and perhaps the most astute scholar in the architecture business today. He has contributed to several books and his two personal efforts, *The Anatomy of a Golf Course* and *The Confidential Guide to Golf Courses*, have been landmark efforts in the recent design "renaissance." In "Play It as It Lies," Mr. Doak confronts some of biggest misnomers in golf architecture, including minimalism, the purpose of hazards and what constitutes real shotmaking.

G.S.

~

Play It as It Lies

by Tom Doak

It's actually Rule 13-1, but it's the most fundamental tenet of golf—we play the ball as it lies. It's also the reason many see golf as a game which builds character, for it's good practice in life to have to accept responsibility for one's previous actions. You can blame anything you want for your errors—a bird chirping in your backswing, bad karma from a previous life, or just a bad lie—but then you have to go play the next shot from wherever you hit it.

Those running for President would have us believe that the spirit of golf is the American ideal, that we all have to negotiate the same course, and we get what we hit. It all sounds very good. But American golfers are suckers for unrealistic promises, just as voters are. We'll buy any new piece of equipment that promises another 20 yards. Our country clubs spend gratuitously to keep their courses in near-perfect condition. And in recent years, our architects spend millions to enclose and define every shot with mounds, while smoothing down every bump in the fairways, attempting to eliminate blind shots and bad bounces from the game.

The result? Instead of building character, we're raising a generation of coddled "champions" who can't even shrug off a bad lie and dig themselves out a divot.

We see the evidence in major championships and the Ryder Cup, against foreign golfers who grew up on imperfect courses, and learned to deal with them. That's the way the game was invented—the original American ideal, that you can change your own destiny if you'll only work hard enough. In Scotland, the links have no trees to stop a wild shot from being swept by the wind to perdition. But there are also none to stymie a potential recovery.

Since the 1950s, American golf design has gone away from that ideal. We seem to expect the course itself to mete out justice, with water hazards and bunkers placed in "tough but fair" positions; but then, we groom the bunkers to permit easy recoveries. Modern American golf design is modeled on the same principles as our ailing criminal justice system—we build more water hazards [prisons], but they only house the disadvantaged, while the elite receive suspended sentences.

But there are now a handful of American designers who see things differently. We've been called minimalists, but the essence of the movement is not in the limited use of earthmoving so much as a return to golf's original values. These are:

1. One of golf's primary appeals is that it's a natural game, and it's more enjoyable when we are playing against natural hazards.
2. A variety of stances in the fairway is a key challenge of golf, and Nature is much better at providing this variety than the hand of man.
3. Shotmaking—the ability to control the flight of the ball—is the ultimate expression of golfing ability, and soft, flat greens reduce shotmaking to artillery practice.
4. Judgment of the shot is as important as execution, and defining the target areas with artificial mounding reduces the value of judgment. Except for visual barriers to eye-

Photo by Tom Doak

IN NATURAL DUNE BUNKERS SUCH AS AT TENBY, WALES, NEITHER A FAIR LIE NOR A STANCE TO AIM AT THE HOLE CAN BE TAKEN FOR GRANTED.

> sores off-site, earthmoving should be confined to features which come into play in the golf holes.

The sad part is that American golfers have become so used to pandering designs that they don't even understand some minimalist ideas. The whole point of golf architecture is to discover and then present to the player challenging shots inherent in the landscape, but today anything remotely challenging is quickly criticized as "unfair." A green which tilts slightly away from the line of play is a natural challenge unto itself, but many golfers are so accustomed to having all the greens tilted back toward them to "receive a shot" that they believe a fallaway green is a gimmick. Gradually, many of the things which can

Photo by Tom Doak (Doak)

THE EIGHTEENTH GREEN AT STONEWALL IS BUILT AT NATURAL GRADE, BUT BUNKERS TO THE RIGHT, THE CLUBHOUSE TO THE LEFT, AND THE LEFT-TO-RIGHT TILT OF THE GROUND ALL AFFECT BOTH SECOND SHOTS AND CHIPPING.

make a golf hole interesting have been removed from modern designers' palettes. Today, even our best designers seldom produce a great golf hole, because they apply so many standards of "fairness" that all their holes begin to look and play alike. Alister MacKenzie wrote of the same problem in *The Spirit of St. Andrews*: "Today nearly everyone plays a coarse and vulgar pitch which punches a hole in the green. With the exception of the Old Course at St. Andrews and few similar courses, there is rarely any necessity to play any other kind of shot. Golfers are losing the joy of playing the variety of approach shots that were so necessary in the old days."

It's easy to talk about "working with the land," but most architects use the land as an amateur interior decorator uses furniture, as raw material to be moved around the room until everything looks perfect. Many modern designers now pay lip service to minimalism, but then back away by saying that they seldom are given pieces of land with natural features to use, and that the concept is applicable to only 10% of new golf courses. Either they are wrong, or I am very lucky to keep finding land which allows it.

The minimalist's objective is to route as many holes as possible whose main features already exist in the landscape, and accent their strategies without overkilling the number of hazards. Sometimes, though, the best solution for the course as a whole may require major earthmoving on a handful of holes to connect the others. That's minimalism, too. And the key to success in those instances is to move enough earth to make the artificial work appear natural, not to move as little as possible.

In general, though, the minimalist moves earth to reduce severe slopes, not to create them. If you want to judge whether a particular designer is really comfortable in the minimalist style, ask him what he does when a hole has no natural feature to build upon. The real minimalist will respond that he's never faced that situation—he'll always find something, whether it's the length of the hole, or a small hump, existing vegetation, or simply the direction of the prevailing wind—and expand upon that to create an interesting golf hole.

~

Editor's Note
Pete Dye and Green Speeds

Often talked about because of his eccentric and controversial work, Pete Dye is usually forgotten as the man most responsible for changing the direction of golf course design over the last thirty years. With new courses becoming more and more stale during the 1960s, Mr. Dye injected shotmaking, strategy, and originality back into the game. At the same time, he started the so-called design "renaissance" toward architecture with character and mental challenges.

A former insurance salesman who was a fine player in his home state of Indiana, Dye's early work included Crooked Stick in Indiana and The Golf Club outside of Columbus, Ohio. They were the first Dye designs after his famous trip to Scotland when Dye and his wife Alice cultivated many of the ideas that would later become his "design trademarks" (railroad ties, use of native grasses, deep grass-faced bunkers and vast waste areas). Though both courses are "low-profile" by Pete Dye standards today, they were a bold deviation from the often listless work of the '60s by Robert Trent Jones, Dick Wilson and George Fazio.

Mr. Dye's work in the seventies furthered his eccentric ideas. Casa De Campo, which sits on a stunning coastline in the Dominican Republic, is Pete Dye's personal favorite, while 1969's Harbour Town and 1976's Oak Tree Golf Club remain as his most popular work with Tour pros. And just when the golf world thought it had seen everything from Pete Dye, along came the first Tournament Players Course in Sawgrass, Florida. Though it was chastised in the early years for being "unfair," the TPC at Sawgrass has evolved into a favorite of Tour players and elevated The Players Championship into one of golf's elite tournaments.

The list of honored and revered Pete Dye courses has continued to grow: PGA West (Stadium) in the California desert; Long Cove Club on Hilton Head Island; Tennessee's The Honors Course; Blackwolf Run in Wisconsin; The Ocean Course on Kiawah Island; Medalist Club in Florida, and his West Virginia masterpiece that was fourteen years in the making, Pete Dye Golf Club.

Mr. Dye has been one of the most "giving" architects of all time. His wife Alice has made immeasurable contributions to their designs and has been a major influence on improving "ladies" or front tees on golf course designs (which she writes about for this book). Unlike most modern designers who just "throw" the forward tees out in front, the Dyes work to design forward tees to play as strategically as they do from the championship set. Pete and Alice Dye have also trained many promising young architecture students. Among those who got their start with the Dyes: his sons Perry and P.B., Tom Doak, Lee Schmidt, Bill Coore, and Bobby Weed.

In "The Evolution of Green Speeds," Mr. Dye explains his theory on the recent direction we have taken with our putting surfaces, and he makes some very interesting points about the future of design if we keep demanding ridiculously fast green speeds.

G.S.

~

The Evolution of Green Speeds

by Pete Dye

In the early 1950s there was no such thing as the "Stimpmeter" reading for testing the speed of greens. At that time, Oakmont Country Club in Pennsylvania notoriously had the fastest greens in the world, but there was no actual way to measure the speed. So I took some films from the 1953 United States Open at Oakmont when Ben Hogan won, and subsequently the 1962 Open won by Jack Nicklaus to see if I could calculate the green speeds at both Opens.

I did this by measuring the time it took the ball to get to the hole and then going out to Oakmont to see where the pin locations were and checking my results on today's greens (the contours have not been altered). The issue of green speeds during the '50s was of great interest to me because I had qualified for the 1957 U.S. Open at Donald Ross' Inverness and remember having many slick putts. And we have all heard the stories of Sam Snead and Hogan talking about how fast Oakmont's greens were, even though they were probably only being cut at a 1/4 inch height, which many of today's courses use as their fringe mowing height!

So I wondered how in the world could they have greens with so much speed cut at only 1/4 of an inch. Well, at that height, the grass blades grow longer, meaning they can collect more sunlight and water, and thus have stronger, deeper roots. And when you have strong roots, you can turn the water off and really dry a green out, meaning they will be nice and firm for a tournament. On top of that, they would roll the greens during the Open, pushing the "grain" or longer bladed grass down in one direction.

When you got putts downhill, down grain, and on dried out greens you got lightning fast putts. And when you went uphill, or into the grain, the putts were frighteningly slow. So on today's Stimpmeter reading, which measures the speed in two directions and takes the average of that, the reading might have been 11 feet one way and 3 the other direction, giving you an average in the neighborhood of 7 feet.

The grain did several things. Agronomically it allowed roots to be stronger and therefore let the superintendent dry the greens out without worrying about losing them. Second, it added all sorts of elements to the game. It required more skill to read the grain on the greens and added more strategy for the approach shots because the grain dictated where you wanted to putt from. So the greens were more difficult to putt, more interesting to approach to, and most of all, a lot easier to maintain.

When Nicklaus came along—and he can tell you—those Oakmont greens were lightning fast again. Yet, they were still rolled and cut at around 1/4 of an inch during the 1962 Open. And if you took a Stimpmeter reading of them, I dare say they were over 7 feet. But if you tell someone that today who played there in '62, they can't believe it because they'll say, "I was there, and I putted off some of those greens." Once again, it was a combination of the same factors: the grain, the dryness, and the rolling that gave the greens their speed in certain directions.

Somewhere between Nicklaus' win at Oakmont and Johnny Miller's in 1973, the Wiehle Roller came out and produced mowing technology where you could cut a green closer (approximately a 3/16 of an inch height). Then in the 1980s, we took another turn and the "groomer" was developed for mowers, which completely changed the way we maintain putting greens.

The groomer acts as a vertical cutting device to help get rid of long bladed grasses and of course, grain. But all this vertical mowing has done is cause headaches for superintendents who do not have the root structure they used to. New technology also increased the power of the mowers and the number of blades, which really took the grain out of the greens. Today, mowing heights go to 1/8 of an inch or less! Add all of that up, and it also happens to be when you started to see so many courses having disease problems with their putting surfaces.

So now we have these vertically cut and thinned out greens with shallow roots that hold up fine for everyday play, but once a tournament comes, the grass can not handle the stress needed to get them up to "championship" conditions. With the shallow roots, and in many cases the new subsurface draining greens, you can only dry the greens out so long before they need water. And once you put water on putting surfaces for the Tour pros, you get "pin cushions" and then you lose another element of shotmaking. Pros just love soft greens because they can get away with mis-hit shots. They can even stop the ball out of the rough or from some place they shouldn't have hit their tee ball!

The other aspect of the game you lose with green speeds averaging somewhere between 11–13 on the Stimpmeter is the ability to build contour into your putting surfaces. Several new grasses have been developed that actually require the mowing height to be a maximum of 1/8 an inch, meaning daily speeds over 11 feet.

If that is the case, no architect in their right mind can build any contour or character into their greens. When you take contour out of the greens and speed them up, you only make the game easier for the average-putting Tour pro, and harder for the club player. There is much more skill required in putting slower, undulating, and grainy greens than there is in putting flat ones that are fast.

So at some point we are going to have to figure out what we really want from our golf courses. Do we want interesting tests of skill with lots of character and perhaps a little grain on the greens? Or do we want level but slick putting surfaces that only make the game less interesting?

~

Editor's Note
Alice Dye and Front Tees

> *While I receive most of the headlines these days for our courses, it is Alice O'Neil Dye who deserves equal credit for any success we've had. There would be not Pete Dye golf courses today if Alice hadn't been by my side.*
>
> —Pete Dye

Elected as the first female President of the American Society of Golf Course Architects in 1997–98, Alice Dye is one of golf architecture's unknown pioneers of the modern era. Pundits love to talk about her husband and his outlandish designs, but lost in all of that chatter is the remarkable contribution of Mrs. Dye in making the game more enjoyable for all players by encouraging better designed "forward" tees.

Both George C. Thomas Jr. and William Flynn took an interest in developing versatile teeing grounds during the 1920s, but it wasn't until Alice Dye in the 1960s and '70s did we see this concept adapted to "front" tees. Many golf courses are simply too hard for ladies, juniors, or senior golfers and the lack of suitable sets of tees discouraged their play. In the following essay, which is used as a reference tool by many modern golf architects, Mrs. Dye lays out the guidelines for designing front tees and how you can create the same strategic design for shorter hitters as you can for the low-handicap golfer.

What makes Mrs. Dye's innovations and standards so remarkable is that she has long been an outstanding golfer who could very easily have ignored such a subject because of her playing prowess. The U.S. Senior Amateur Champion in 1978 and 1979, Mrs. Dye is also a former Curtis Cup team member, North and South Amateur Champion, and nine-time Indiana State champion.

G.S.

~

Adding Tees to Existing Golf Courses

by Alice Dye

Clubs with courses designed by one of the old master architects understandably do not want changes which would affect their identity with that particular architect. However, not realizing many changes have already occurred they are hesitant to add new tees, especially ones that would benefit the weaker players in the club.

Beginning in the 1950s, watering systems began to be installed and many blue grass fairways were replaced with bent grass. Greenside bunkers were drawn around to guard the front of the green and the rear bunkers eliminated. The small trees grew tall and spread out, often overhanging the new smaller fairway and blocking out fairway bunkers. The old bunkers no longer in play were replaced with new ones tightening the landing area. The roll of the ball was reduced and golf became a game played in the air, not to mention that holes now played much longer.

The manufacturers of playing equipment responded with clubs and balls that helped players carry their shots farther in the air, so existing courses have countered by extending their back tees. But players of lesser strength find they do not benefit as much from the new equipment as the stronger players do. Women, juniors, and seniors find that without roll, the holes play too long.

Closely mowed fairways demanded by the low handicappers

also make hitting shots more difficult for the average players. On longer grass, players are able to fly the ball with a sweeping swing but sheered turf requires a stroke that brings the club down through the turf, requiring much more strength and ability. Watering systems have also been extended into the rough areas, taking away their sparse playability and making them thick and lush so that great strength is needed to execute a successful shot. Now, not only does the watering system make the holes play longer, but subtle design changes and highly specialized maintenance have increased the difficulty for the average player.

Today, courses designed by the old master architects no longer play as they were intended and clubs not wanting to "change" their course by adding new tees should realize the big change their watering system, turf, bunkers, trees and green speeds have made over the years. What would their master architect do to his course were he alive? How would he accommodate the vast difference in ability of the members?

The answer is simple: new back tees compensate for better equipment and forward tees should return the playing characteristics and strategy the original architect intended for the average and high handicappers.

Length and Position of Forward Tees

People have to understand that forward tees are not just shortened yardage. Many of the above listed factors need to be considered, most especially condition of turf. The majority of forward tee golfers drive the ball approximately 130 yards on the typical watered fairway. Architects have extended the length of holes for stronger players and should provide shorter yardage for those with less strength. Shorter yardage is not meant to take the challenge out of the game. Instead, its goal should be to adapt the playing characteristics of the holes to the ability of the player.

USGA Suggested Yardages

	Women	**Men**
Par 3	up to 211	up to 250
Par 4	212 to 240	251 to 475
Par 5	401 to 575	475 and up
Par 6	575 and up	

Alice Dye's Suggestions for Forward Tees

Par 3	9 to 150
Par 4	230 to 340
Par 5	401 to 430
Par 6	AVOID

Another very serious objection to adding front tees is the fear that players using them will have their handicaps go down. It is difficult for players to understand that their lower scores on a shortened course will not lower their handicap index. All sets of tees are rated and "Sloped," and scores are figured on the tee played, and then adjusted accordingly. They must understand that their handicap index will not change and that when they play a more difficult course they will be given additional strokes.

High Course and Slope Ratings and a high Stimpmeter reading for greens have become ridiculous status symbols. The Course rating from each tee is a number the scratch player would shoot if he played perfectly. The Slope rating is not a measure of the difficulty of the course but rather a measure of the difficulty of the course for an average player compared to the difficulty of the scratch player.

A course like Augusta National would have a high Course rating but not have a high Slope rating because it does not play that much tougher for the average player than it does for the scratch player. The fairways are wide, there is no rough, and the scratch player has equal difficulty on the pitched greens. Crooked Stick and PGA West would have high Slope ratings because the average player would have serious problems with the forced carries and length from the back tees.

So a high Slope rating is only a number showing how players using tees unmanageable for them would play in relation to a scratch player using the same back tees. It is much more prestigious to have a Slope rating between 126–136 because it reveals that you have a challenging, but fair golf course, and isn't that what we all really want?

~

Editor's Note
Hanse and Fieldwork

Another rising young architect who is basing his work on the principles of classic architecture, Gil Hanse became just the third American architect to build a course in Scotland. Mr. Hanse recently spent almost a year in the home of golf, "hand crafting" the 18-hole Craighead Golf Links for the Crail Golfing Society, the world's seventh oldest golf club.

Mr. Hanse has been involved in several important restoration and long-range planning projects. He has begun to lay out a master plan for Merion near his home in Philadelphia, as well as oversee restoration work at several other classic courses including Kittansett Club in Massachusetts, William Flynn's Lancaster Country Club in Pennsylvania, and Herbert Strong's Engineers Club in New York.

In "Designing in the Field," Hanse details the importance of on-site design and construction. Fieldwork, or a lack thereof, is the most obvious difference between the work undertaken during the Golden Age of golf design and today's architecture.

G.S.

~

Designing in the Field

by Gil Hanse

There appears to be no small movement afoot to embrace the ideals, principles and characteristics of the golf course architects from the Golden Age of design. We read so much about them and their approaches, and so many architects have adroitly rehearsed all of the catch phrases that can be associated with these magnificent men. However, as we celebrate their accomplishments, we drift farther and farther from the true heart and soul of their work.

Golf course architecture, along with its sister profession, golf course maintenance, has become more sterile in its approach to the design, construction, and maintenance of golf courses than ever before. We take a fine tooth comb and rake it over the construction specifications and maintenance programs of our golf courses. Architects have become more concerned with particle sizes than with natural settings for golf holes, and there is just as much emphasis placed on cart path location as on bunker location. Cut and fill calculations have replaced the most subtle adjustments for style and character. We profess to hold the ideals of these architects in our hearts; however, when it comes to practicing these ideals there are only a handful of architects who truly do so.

It is my belief that to truly do justice to the ideals of men like Macdonald, Tillinghast, Flynn, and MacKenzie, the architect must concentrate on designing in the field. It is only there that the true nature of the golf course site will make itself evident to the designer. All of these gentlemen spent considerable amounts of time in the field. It is evident in their work and in their ability to extract all that was possible out of the natural features of the site. The master architects felt the site in their hearts, and they studied it with a keen eye. They got their hands on it, observed it in different lights, in different moods. They related to the site. To the modern, sterile architect who is contented by looking at the site from the front seat of a Range Rover, this may indeed seem an odd concept. However, it is at the heart of what the masters believed and what they practiced.

In our search for better science, a lot of these theories got left by the wayside. Why should any architect have to saddle himself with one or two projects, when six or seven could be had? With modern transportation and standardized construction techniques, an architect could easily make an appearance on site once every two weeks and "guarantee" that any particular golf course would be unique. This has led to the franchise mentality which plagues so much of golf course architecture, producing a sameness to many layouts built during the last twenty years. This is a function of the fact that golf course architects, after reaching a certain level of fame, spend more and more of their time on sales and marketing, and less on design. As a result, there is a tendency to rely on what has worked in the past and to shy away from the unconventional or the innovative.

Golf course architecture of this nature cannot be any farther removed from the ideals of the Golden Age. Through their utilization of natural features and their presence on site, the masters created golf holes that were exciting, challenging, and certainly innovative. By being on site for an extended period of time, the architect can mold the land to accomplish whatever effects he desires. There must always be a certain amount of artistic license that any architect should bring to his work. This license can best be employed through an intimate knowledge of the site and an equally intimate knowledge of the classic examples of architecture passed down by the master architects. Having this experience can allow the architect to make changes in the field that will produce a more interesting golf course.

By observing construction, the golf architect will perhaps be struck by how something looks at a certain stage of earth moving. It may strike a cord with him that it is reminiscent of a feature he has observed elsewhere, and that implementing this feature here could be the perfect fit for the golf course. This observation would be impossible to make once everything was given its final shape. In this respect, designing in the field allows the architect a longer period of time to study and reflect upon the golf course design. In this fast-paced profession, that would undoubtedly be a good thing for most every architect.

Of course, there are practicalities which need to be addressed like budgets and plans for the golf course. I am not suggesting that designers simply be allowed to wing it in the field. However, I do believe firmly that through constant observation and through working with the land, any architect would have the opportunity to be more creative with his design, adding subtle touches that would greatly enhance the interest of the golf course. As for the budget, it has been my experience that a conscientious architect, working with a dedicated contractor, can more than make up for the cost of field changes through the added efficiency of a project where the on-site architect is making instantaneous design and construction decisions.

Designing in the field can take on so many connotations,

and every architect has his own comfort level with his on-site involvement. It is my belief that designing in the field means spending at least half of the days on site that a golf course is under construction. This is indeed a major commitment for any golf course architect to make. However, it was not too much of a commitment for C.B. Macdonald at The National Golf Links of America, nor was it too much of a commitment for Hugh Wilson at Merion. In fact the list of examples goes on and on, and it shows that most of the "great" golf courses in this country were created with the architect on site for the majority of the project.

By designing in the field the architect is in control of the outcome. The results are not an interpretation of his work, but rather a literal representation of his ideas and creativity. By get-

Photo by Gil Hanse *(Gil Hanse)*

THE 480-YARD FIRST AT CRAIGHEAD GOLF LINKS, CRAIL, SCOTLAND BEFORE FINAL SEEDING. A MODEST OPENING THREE-SHOTTER WITH A GREEN REMINISCENT OF THE ROAD HOLE.

Photo by Jim Horsfield *(Gil Hanse)*

AERIAL VIEW OF THE CRAIGHEAD GOLF LINKS, CRAIL, SCOTLAND BEFORE OPENING. MR. HANSE DESIGNED THIS COURSE "IN THE FIELD."

ting their hands back onto projects, I believe that we could again see a renaissance in the beauty, character, and natural splendor of golf courses. We would also see a dramatic increase in the subtleties and nuances that have made the brilliant designs of the Golden Age so charming, strategic, and above all, interesting to play.

It is very difficult for an equipment operator, or even the most experienced shaper to add these brush strokes to the canvas, and even if they could, it would be their touch rather than that of the architect. If an artist were to have a vision for a painting, it would indeed be most effective for him to paint it by himself. However, he could train someone to do the painting for him, and through careful instruction and daily supervision come up with a painting very near to the original vision. Imagine the difficulty he would have, if he were to train that person

Photo by Gil Hanse *(Gil Hanse)*

THE 375-YARD NINTH AT CRAIGHEAD GOLF LINKS, CRAIL, SCOTLAND
BEFORE FINAL SEEDING

and then go away for two weeks, only to return and find that the painting was not quite what he had in mind. In this case, it would either be "good enough," or it would have to be changed and the apprentice would have to start over. We work with bigger canvases in our field, yet we should be artists in the way we manipulate and shape our golf courses. It is only through constant attention and designing in the field that we will come up with the true vision we had intended for, rather than something that is merely "good enough." We can be sure that Alister MacKenzie and George Thomas never settled for anything less than perfection.

It is unfortunate that the rebirth or rediscovery of the talented golf course architects of the Golden Age is coinciding with a period of architecture that is generally far removed from the principles that they espoused. Through the use of computers, science, and modern transportation it has become much more convenient and lucrative to focus on quantity rather than quality. My dear friend and colleague, Bill Kittleman, sums it up so succinctly when he says about modern design: "there just isn't a whole lot of home cooking anymore, everything is microwaved." Let us hope that before we forget the home cooking recipes which made golf course architecture great, we can restore the principles that were left to us by embracing our sites and working hard in the field to squeeze every ounce of character, strategy, and natural interest out of the landscape.

~

Editor's Note
Forse and Trees

One our few true restoration experts, Ron Forse has seen countless American golf courses that are overwrought with unnecessary trees. The saddest trend of post World War II architecture was the recommendation by many architects to plant trees, or worse, use them as a hazard.

The master architects' experience came primarily from the architecture of the British Isles where trees are virtually never used as a hazard. Only recently in this country have any architects been successful in convincing green committees of the need to remove unnecessary specimens.

Mr. Forse has overseen restorations and long-range master plans at several important Donald Ross original designs, including Salem and Brae Burn Country Clubs in Massachusetts. Based in Uniontown, Pennsylvania, he has also coordinated restoration work at original designs by William Flynn, A.W. Tillinghast, and William Langford. He is also a frequent lecturer to superintendents about preparing master plans and has delivered seminars on various subjects of architecture and planning, including his most popular, "To Tree or Not to Tree."

G.S.

~

To Tree or Not to Tree

by Ron Forse

There are few things in nature which give us as much enjoyment as a beautiful, mature tree. Who is not awestruck by a giant, gnarly White Oak? And who can pass a huge multi-trunked Banyan Ficus tree without stopping to take in the sight? Trees are one of God's marvelous creations. They are also an integral part of the American landscape and thus an ingredient in our golf course settings.

However, there has been nothing more destructive to the architecture of golf courses than poorly planted trees. Our courses are intended to be places where the game of golf can be played in its most enjoyable state. They are not supposed to be arboretums where we're so asphyxiated that it's difficult to take the club back because of towering pines lining the fairway.

George C. Thomas Jr., who gave us several fine courses in the Los Angeles area, succinctly described the importance of proper tree planting: "Trees and shrubbery beautify the course, and natural growth should never be cut down if it is possible to save it; but he who insists on preserving a tree where it spoils a shot should have nothing to say about golf course construction."

The courses are legion where the original design intent and strategies have been altered or nullified by trees. Often these are the result of so-called "course beautification" programs, but often they end up ruining the charm of the original design.

Master architects like Mr. Thomas or Alister MacKenzie would have much to say to the green committees who have blanketed their original designs with tall woody plants of all sorts. And rightly so, because the single greatest factor in altering the character of their masterpieces has been what the Scots call "bunkers in the sky."

Golf courses should predominantly be designed and built around ground features, whether they be the existing natural topography or man-made features such as bunkers and swales. Golf courses should not be designed around trees. Ben Crenshaw once said that what he loves most about Augusta National is that it allows "full expression of recovery." The wide corridors between the tree-lined fairways enable stray shots to still be played off turf instead of punched sideways out of trees.

Dr. MacKenzie's wonderful design at Augusta National, though extensively altered, still remains in spirit because Augusta places such a premium on strategic play by creating preferred and not-so-preferred sides of the fairway from which to approach the putting surfaces. If trees were planted directly on the sides of the fairways it would cut off the various strategic routes from tee to green. One could name a multitude of real life examples to show this, and suffice to say that almost every classic course in America has suffered this malady to one degree or another.

One of the principal aspects of a good golf course is that it is strategic. Without alternate routes to the green, a golf hole becomes one-dimensional and takes on the characteristic of just one repetitive avenue of playing the hole. And once our golf holes lose their interest and only reward the physically superior, the true thrill of the game is lost.

Trees and new "forward" tees are the two most controversial

topics when planning improvements for existing courses, with trees being the hot button issue at virtually every course I visit. When it is recommended to remove a tree because of its interference in the play of a hole, or its root competition with the surrounding turf, or with its casting too much shade on the grass beneath, one would think that you were trying to kill someone's Aunt Millie! Matters get really sticky when the club in question has implemented a memorial tree program over the years. One can barely trim trees planted under these auspices, let alone cut one down!

It is also a common misconception that one should *not* see another golf hole from the one which you are playing. Cutting off a vista violates the enjoyment of views across the golf property. Aren't golf courses supposed to be beautiful places? Why should tree lines choke every vista and close them off? Anyone who has visited Augusta National, Baltusrol, or Riviera, will tell you that the wonderful open sections in front of the clubhouses not only create a beautiful view of the approaching fairways, but also lend variety to what are otherwise tree-lined courses.

Well-designed tree planting programs, a most rare breed indeed, appear indigenous. Trees must be arranged in such a way that they do not portray mans' hand in their arrangement. Every feature of a golf course should be entirely natural and fit with the existing topography of the property. Most of all, if you are going to plant trees, place them in groves and always avoid the "row" effect, for there is nothing less natural than a straight line of pines you could tie a line to and hang laundry from!

H.S. Colt, the British architect who gave Alister MacKenzie his start in the architecture business, once stated that trees "are a fluky and obnoxious hazard." Colt's description is most

The American Golfer *(Crump and Colt)*

THE 424-YARD PAR-4 EIGHTEENTH AT PINE VALLEY, CIRCA 1925.

Photo by Lynn Shackelford *(Crump and Colt)*

THE SAME HOLE TODAY. EITHER WAY YOU FEEL ABOUT TREES, IT IS STILL A REMARKABLE HOLE.

appropriate when trees have been used for the purpose of making golf holes more difficult. A fine example of how not to plant a tree can be seen at the corner of many once-classic dogleg holes. Where the bunkering on the inside of the turn has become too easy to carry for the tee shot, the inexpensive "remedy" quite often is seen to be tree planting. And usually the fast growing type is picked, producing an inferior focal point for the hole.

Bunkering the inside of a dogleg creates strategic playing options. One can carry or play around the bunker or try to run the ball along its edge. Trees in lieu of bunkering or other such ground features force the hole to be played essentially in one way: away from the corner of the dogleg. This is a common mistake and a classic example of how strategy is snatched from a hole with the planting of just a few trees. The real solution to accommodate new equipment and longer-hitting golfers is to extend the tee or continue the bunkering or other topographic features further from the tee, thus maintaining the original strategy and shot value.

All this is *not* to say that one should never use a tree as part of a hole's design. There are many beautiful examples where trees are an integral part of the strategy, such as at the famed 17th at Cypress Point. These strategically placed trees must be long-lasting and beautiful in their own right, otherwise, they are useless and at some point the hole becomes susceptible to drastic change should lightning or disease strike them dead.

Trees are also very useful in framing views across a landscape. They are advantageous as backdrops for green sites but this has also been sadly overdone in modern times. The putting surface, its contrasting bunkers, and the surrounding topography are almost always enough to give "definition." The idea of using trees to add depth perception is fine from time to time, but how often we see it grossly overworked to the point where committees, or even architects, forget the agronomic headaches created when the trees become fully grown.

On this agronomic side, trees should never be planted so that important parts of the east or southeast sides on the golf course are severely covered. It is vital that the morning sun be allowed to reach the ground so the soil can warm up. This allows the turf to grow throughout the day, thereby helping it to recover from stress and damage. Our tall wooded friends should also never be planted too close to greens, and shallow rooted trees, which bring so many safety problems with them, simply have no place on a golf course. Green committees are often absent-minded to sunlight issues and this is where a qualified superintendent or golf architect is vital in directing a tree planting program.

With trees, often less is more. It's better to have a few well-spaced and developed trees planted with room to mature, than a multitude of spindly trunks crowding themselves out for sunlight. Too often, short-sighted tree planting programs want quick results with weaker, faster growing trees instead of purchasing heartier specimens that will last for generations.

We must also remember that trees simply are not necessary in the design of a golf course. Many of the best layouts in the world do not rely on trees in their design scheme and some such as the Old Course at St. Andrews, or Shinnecock Hills and Sand Hills Golf Club here in America, do not rely on them at all. Many American country clubs are beginning to see the benefits of eliminating hundreds of trees, not only for their maintenance budgets, but also in improving the enjoyment of their golf course. One of our truly classic tournament venues, Oakmont Country Club outside of Pittsburgh, Pennsylvania, has removed nearly fifteen hundred trees in the last five years. The original "rugged" look of Oakmont had been preserved until the death of the course's co-architect W.C. Fownes. Sometime after he passed away in 1949, the roughs were planted with thousands of trees. The current committees at Oakmont discovered that three key features of the course were enhanced by the removal of trees: (1) the return of some freedom to recover from poor shots and hazards, (2) improved agronomic conditions, and (3) restoration of the original, superior design.

Oakmont's bold tree removal program is a good model in recognizing that we do not need thousands of trees on our American courses to make them more interesting. On the contrary, fewer trees only ease the burden placed on the club's maintenance budget, enhance the strategy of a well-designed hole, and reward the expert player who can create skillful recovery shots.

~

Editor's Note
Coore and the Boys

Bill Coore's passion for architecture began while playing Perry Maxwell's Old Town Club and Donald Ross's Pinehurst during his college days at North Carolina's Wake Forest. Like so many other talented architects today, Coore joined Pete Dye and Associates for ten years before starting his own firm in 1982. After several highly regarded efforts, including Rockport Country Club in Texas and Golf du Medoc in France, Coore joined forces with Ben Crenshaw in 1986.

Besides their idyllic design at Sand Hills Golf Club in Mullen, Nebraska, Coore and Crenshaw have taken their strategic design style to the Plantation Course at Kapalua, 18-holes at Barton Creek in their hometown of Austin, Texas, and a 9-hole addition to historic Southern Hills in Tulsa, Oklahoma. They have also undertaken several high-profile restorations, including A.W. Tillinghast's Brook Hollow in Dallas, Texas and George Thomas' Riviera Country Club in Pacific Palisades, California.

But it's their 1997 work at Talking Stick in golf-rich Scottsdale, Arizona, that prompted Mr. Coore to write the following essay. "In Tribute to the Boys" is Bill Coore's ode to the men who do the real work in golf course design. And although this book serves as a celebration of the "master" architects and their work, we must not forget the thousands of men, boys, and horses who constructed the great courses from the past. "In Tribute to the Boys" is Mr. Coore's way of thanking the men who work for him while giving the reader an insider's view of how a golf course project really works.

G.S.

~

In Tribute to the Boys

by Bill Coore

It's spring in the desert. I'm out for a walk, a tour of Talking Stick, the 36-hole complex that our company is designing in Scottsdale, Arizona. "The boys," as Ben Crenshaw and I respectfully refer to the men who are our associates, are hard at work.

Even after twenty-five years in this business, I'm amazed at what is happening here. The two courses begun in August are contoured into shape. The North Course is approaching the grassing stage.

I'm walking, alone with my thoughts, feeling so very proud of the work that these men are doing; and let there be no mistake, "the boys" are the ones doing it. I'm looking at work that could not possibly have been defined on paper. I'm looking at the product of years of experience brought together as a unit.

Teamwork is a beautiful thing. Everyone in the right place, at the right time; each individual doing what he knows best; each exhibiting his own immense talent, yet each mindful, respectful and appreciative of the other men and the other talents around him.

In any direction that I turn or at any contour I look, I see these men's individual artistry. They are taking Ben's and my conceptual input and bringing it to life. They are the designers of these courses ever as much as we are.

Designing and constructing a golf course is an evolutionary

process. It is a process of starting with an idea, a concept, and then adapting to the changes that occur to that concept in the field.

Ben and I try to convey the proposed themes and strategy of the course. Sometimes, these are in specific terms regarding angles or contours of greens, bunkers, or fairways. More often, we ask the boys to just start building something based upon our conceptual conversations and sketches. They give us something to look at, something to edit, refine or abandon. At times, they create something totally different than what we expected or perhaps desired. Often, this new feature is better than what we originally envisioned. Together the boys and we adapt, learn, and create. We understand one another. It is an understanding born of years of communication and side by side work.

For too long now, the myth has been perpetuated that the architect of record does all the design of a golf course. With all due respect to the people in my profession, many of whom are extraordinarily talented, let me state emphatically that is not the case. The all encompassing "I" in this business does not exist. We, the architects, are merely a piece of the puzzle that must be assembled to create a golf course. In our experience, that has never been more true than here at Talking Stick, our first foray into golf in the desert.

Rarely have we encountered a site so devoid of natural features for golf. We who take pride in selecting sites readily adaptable to golf, found ourselves standing in the midst of four hundred acres of flat desert floor; one percent grade throughout. The human eye cannot detect a one percent change in elevation.

Routing the courses at Talking Stick was relatively easy. Basically treeless as well as flat, the holes could go in any direction. There was nothing on the site; no severity, no permitting condition that determined either concept or availability. It was a blank canvas upon which we attempted to lay thirty-six holes, many of which we had long wanted to build but never had the opportunity.

Purely conceptual in nature, the routings seemed ideal. After all, we had been given free rein. "Do anything you like," said Dana Germany, the president of Troon North Golf Management, the company representing the Pima Maricopa Indian Community for whom we are working. "All we ask is that you create two golf courses different from any in the desert and make each one distinctively different from the other." It was a rather serious challenge on land of one percent grade.

We were going to need the boys.

In July of 1996, Ben, Dave Axland (our design associate) and I walked the staked routings. It was a cloudless, dusty day well above one hundred degrees. It was a preview of days to come.

We came face to face with the reality of the job at hand. One staked hole followed another and another, each just as lifeless in its natural state as the preceding one.

Later, Ron Despain, the engineering guru who was to guide us throughout this project explained that the work would be made more difficult by the nature of the soil. Collapsible soil he called it; a new term for Dave, Ben and me. We listened, not happily, as he described a type of soil that could not be compacted or shaped into any lasting form without first being mixed with water; and just the right amount of water at that. It was a difficult task, he said. We came to realize that Ron was a master of understatement.

"Drainage," Ron said, "will be critical. But you can do anything you want; any kind of holes that you want, as long as we can figure out how to build them and drain them." We knew then that we were going to need the boys, all of them, if possible.

It's spring in the desert and they're here. With the exception of Tom Beck, Dan Proctor, and Jim Lyles, everyone with whom Ben and I have worked since the inception of our company is here.

I'm walking, watching and admiring. J. Colson Clarke, better known as "Scrooge," is grading the contours of a fairway with a 6-ton, D-6 bulldozer, making each movement appear as natural as though Mother Nature herself were at the controls.

In the world of golf course construction, the men who operate massive machines that contour the landscape into features suitable for golf are known as shapers. In reality, they are sculptors, artists of the earth, the very best of whom are capable of taking the most sketchy of plans from an architect and transforming them into an artistic and functioning reality.

Steady and reassuring in mood, manner, and work, Scrooge (with whom I have worked for nearly twenty years) is the cornerstone of the crew. He is a teacher who has helped guide and influence all who have come after him.

Across the way I see Mike McKay, the second shaper to join us in 1982. He is roughing in yet another green. A man of few words and many talents, our conversations usually go something like, "That looks great, Mike."

James "Jimbo" Wright is the product of the experience of Scrooge, Mike, and his own incredible talents honed by eight years of working in this business. As a detail shaper, Jimbo is capable of creating contours of greens that could be grassed without further refinement. His is a sense of artistic feel and mechanical skill equal to any.

Further along, I see Jeff Bradley and a small crew of men working on a bunker on the North Course. Jeff's creations are not merely bunkers to fulfill a function, but lacy edged masterpieces right out of a Tom Simpson sketchbook. They are works of art.

Jim Craig is organizing the finish crew in preparation for grass. Talking Stick is his first project with us. It won't be his last. Seldom have I seen a man capable of doing so many things so well. Peter Reille, the man in charge of the South Course, is busy preparing for the impending onslaught of irrigation, drainage, and finish crews heading in his direction. An aspiring architect, Peter wanted to work with us because he heard that we do things differently. We needed Pete's abilities as a technician; he needed to see how courses could be created more by feel than formula. We are learning from each other.

Dave Axland, our company's on-site design representative, drives by in a dusty pick- up truck. More than any other single person, Dave deserves the credit for the creation of Talking Stick. So much of the field design has been a product of his experience and imagination. Additionally, he has had to be the man in charge of the technicalities of construction of both courses. Incredibly, he has even managed to spend time on a bulldozer being "creative."

I climb atop a stockpile of dirt. Far in the distance, a solitary bulldozer rumbles in the dust. It is Rod Whitman, one of my dearest friends for over twenty years and an accomplished golf architect in his own right. He has personally designed courses in Canada, France, and Germany and collaborated with Ben and me in Indonesia. At Talking Stick, Rod and his brother

Tim have been the lead dozer men, roughing in holes for Scrooge, Mike, and Jimbo. Rod's facility for grasping a design concept and creating contours that bring it to life is proof that there are a few architects who can actually build as well as draw something.

Earlier, Dave had asked about Tom Beck. Tom is in Notre Dame, Indiana, where he will be the design associate for our project on campus there. He's busy with the clearing of the course, but having known and worked with Tom for fourteen years, I know that he is feeling left out. He knows what is happening here in the desert.

Dan Proctor was here. He supervised the bulk dirt work placement last summer. Another proven architect, his design experience was invaluable in the initial placement of the dirt, which in turn made all of our subsequent jobs easier.

It's near sunset, the end of the day. As I walk into the construction yard, I see the boys, dusty and tired standing together at the back of a pick-up. They're talking about Scott Sayers our business partner. "Where's Scotty when you need him?" Scrooge asks as I walk by.

"Probably in some nice air conditioned restaurant sipping champagne," I reply. They all laugh. They know differently. He is probably somewhere fretting about whether these men are going to have work next year. Scotty is definitely one of the boys.

Dave wants me to ride out onto the North Course to look at grassing lines. As we slowly make our way, the slanting light reveals minute contours that were imperceptible earlier in the day.

"Scrooge's work," Dave says quietly.

At one point he turns to me and says, "Bill I know that this project has been as difficult as any we've ever done and I'm probably prejudiced, but is it as good as I think it is?"

"Yes, Dave, it is. It's a clinic on how to create a golf course on flat ground; and Dave, it's a tribute to the boys."

"It may not happen again," he says, "all these guys in one place at one time."

"I know."

~

Editor's Note
Maintaining Hazards

As the editor, I have subtly (or not so subtly) embedded my own opinions throughout this book, but the following essay is my chance to come right out and say what's on my mind. I selected hazard maintenance because it is one of the most backward and bizarre trends in modern golf architecture.

G.S.

~

How Hazards Should Be Maintained

by Geoff Shackelford

haz•ard *(haz'erd) noun A chance of being injured or harmed; danger.*

Without hazards, golf would have become extinct long ago. By hazards, we mean bunkers, creeks, lakes, swamps, barrancas, ravines, tall grasses, waste areas—you get the idea.

No component of golf architecture is more important than the incorporation of hazards into the design. Several essays in this book explain how hazards should be placed to improve the interest of the course architecture, but none of the articles defines how our hazards should be maintained. Perhaps that's because none of the master architects could have imagined that golf course maintenance would become such a highly refined science. Unfortunately, golf course maintenance, especially in the United States, has become so exceptional that our hazards are actually maintained *too well*. Uniformity, as opposed to irregularity, has rendered many a wonderfully placed hazard pointless.

The most obvious shift has been in bunker maintenance. Today's golfer expects a perfect lie each and every time they are in the sand. Though I have no problem with bunkers being raked on a daily basis, there is nothing more pathetic than the post-shot pleading of a Tour player who is begging that his ball land in a bunker instead of the four-inch rough on either side of that bunker. Isn't it ridiculous that bunkers are becoming a better place to be than the rough?

Why even have bunkers if they are friendly and the tall grass our enemy? Bunkers were placed on a course to wreak havoc; grass is planted as a playing surface. Yet, the "Championship" or "Tournament" quality course is now defined and maintained as one where the grass wreaks the havoc and the bunkers provide breathing room. The USGA, in a desperate attempt to preserve the importance of hazards at Baltusrol for the 1993 U.S. Open, wisely ended its bunker maintenance practices (watering and packing down) so that the rough would not ruin the intentions of Mr. Tillinghast's hazards. On the other end of the spectrum, I have watched crews water down the bunkers at my home course in preparation for a Tour event, and even add tennis court clay to harden up the sand!

This is not to say I advocate C.B. Macdonald's belief that elephants be allowed to "run wild in the bunkers." You want to give golfers a chance to recover from a hazard, otherwise skillful and imaginative players go unnoticed. However, bunker conditions must be irregular enough to create all sorts of lies—some good, some bad, and some that are just plain unpredictable. It should require creativity and talent to recover from a hazard, not complete luck.

The Tour goes to great lengths to make bunker sand as firm as possible so that their players hit dynamic spinning shots, leaving the crowd in awe. This is all fine and wonderful, but don't tell me that we are doing justice to the architecture of classic courses by making the bunkers more ideal than the rough. And judging by the recent success of international players in the major championships—who grow up playing in adverse and sometimes downright weird conditions—the Tour is not doing its players a whole lot of justice.

A similar kind of "ironic hazard maintenance" briefly occurred at Augusta National on the wonderful par-5 thirteenth. For many years the creek fronting the green was a combination of trickling water, pebbles, grass, and an occasional sand bar. This "irregularity" added to the temptations of a player who was not sure whether to risk going for the green in two shots. By having the chance of danger in its irregular state, and also the chance of recovery, the hazard in front of #13 created major headaches for the best players in the world. But a few years ago, someone decided the hole would be better served if the creek were filled with several feet of water, thus eliminating the opportunity for those occasional recovery shots. They also thought they were making the short par-5 more difficult.

Raising the water level actually made the hole simpler for the best players in the world. Yes, more simple. By creating a creek with no hope of recovery, a good player who was 235 yards away from a hanging lie had virtually no temptation to go for the green. His decision was already made for him. But with an unpredictable creek, and the off-chance he could miss the green and still end up on the bank or sitting pretty on a sand bar, that same player will probably try to reach the green in two shots. Thankfully, the braintrust at Augusta National, who otherwise do a superb job every year presenting a true and "firm" test of golf, have partially restored this irregular element to the creek on #13 and it is once again tempting the best golfers in the world each April.

So how should hazards be maintained? They should be irregular, unpredictable, and dangerous. They should not be easy, nor should they be maintained in a way that their only purpose

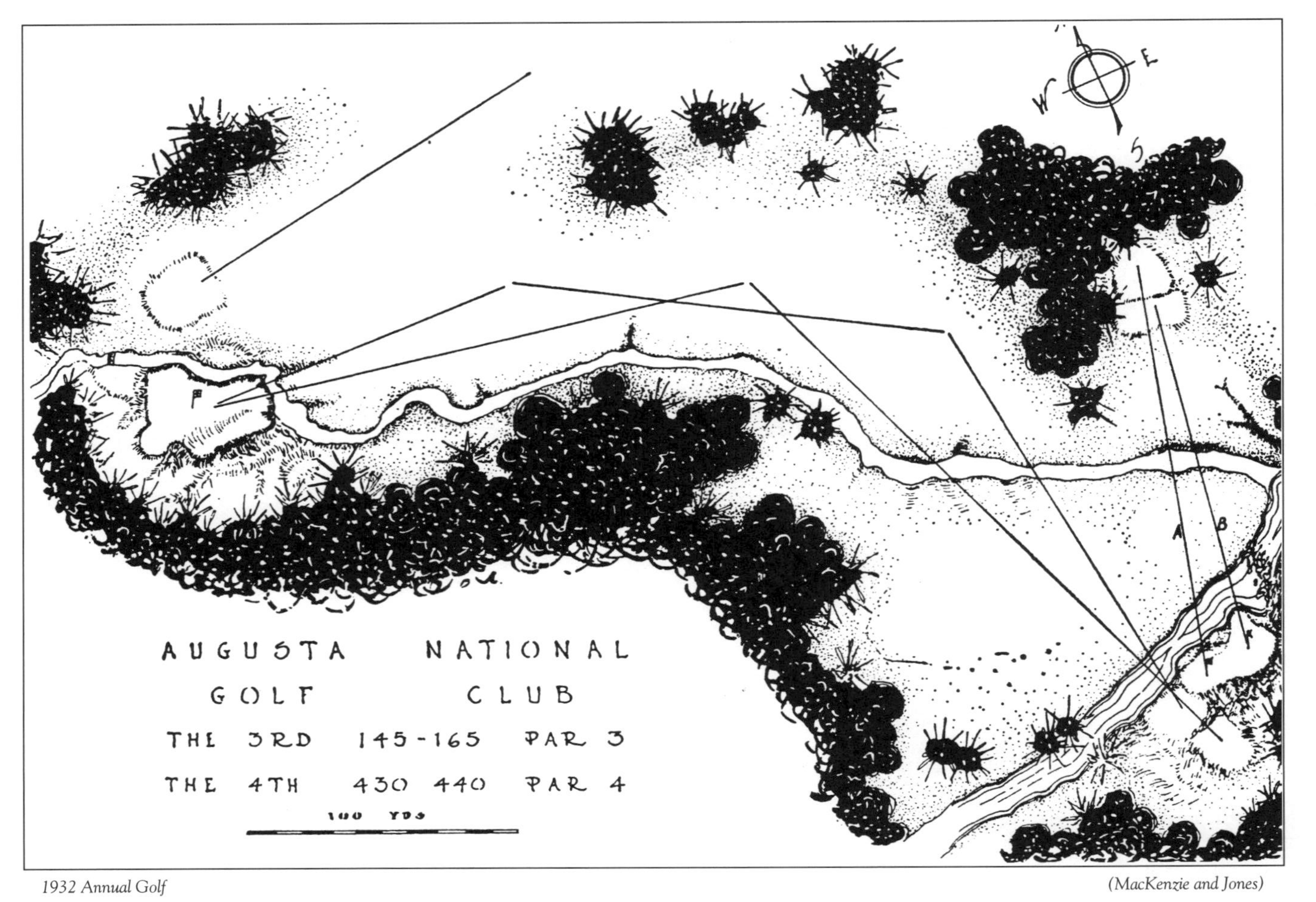

1932 Annual Golf *(MacKenzie and Jones)*

DR. MACKENZIE'S ORIGINAL SKETCH OF THE PAR-5 THIRTEENTH AT AUGUSTA NATIONAL. AS BEN CRENSHAW SAYS, "IT ENCOMPASSES EACH OF THE THREE SCHOOLS OF GOLF COURSE ARCHITECTURE: STRATEGIC, PENAL, AND HEROIC."

is to swallow up golf balls and force the golfer to take an unplayable lie drop. Giving the player an opportunity to recover not only makes the game more fun, but also makes the decision making process just that much more interesting. Because if you take away the mental dilemmas of a sport and make it a merely a test of physical skill, it becomes stereotyped and ultimately ruins the joy of that sport.

~

Editor's Note
Weed and Faster Play

There may be no greater problem plaguing golf today than slow play, and some even feel that it threatens the growth of golf in the future. Florida-based architect Bobby Weed brings an architect's more practical approach to architecture and maintenance in his essay, "Design for Speed."

Several factors are usually blamed for the increased time it takes to play a round, but Mr. Weed is one of the few architects to actually speak out and advocate ways to improve the situation without compromising the strategy and intrigue of our courses. After building his own practice bunker and green on his father's farm, a young Bobby Weed met Pete and Alice Dye during summer work at Amelia Island Plantation. Mr. Dye hired Bobby Weed in 1980 to work on Hilton Head Island's Long Cove Club where he learned the various aspects of the business that made Dye successful. Soon after, he was hired as the Golf Course Superintendent at the TPC at Sawgrass, where Weed would work over several years to improve the original TPC design with Dye's consent.

His work at Sawgrass led to a promotion by the PGA Tour to construction superintendent for all TPC courses, and just a few years later Weed was spending all of his time as lead designer of the future TPC courses. Among the courses Weed designed with various Tour pros are the TPCs at Tampa Bay, River Highlands in Connecticut, a co-design with Pete Dye on the TPC at Sawgrass-Valley Course, and two courses at Summerlin in Las Vegas. Weed has since left the Tour to create his own firm, and his early solo work includes a restoration of Donald Ross's Timuquana Country Club in Jacksonville.

G.S.

~

Design for Speed

by Bobby Weed

I recently had a conversation with the legendary Gene Sarazen and during our visit he voiced great concern regarding today's "pace of play." Imagine playing a round of golf fifty years ago with knee-high rough, maybe only a shrub to indicate the 150-yard mark to greens, and once you reached the putting surfaces, they were all remarkably inconsistent. By today's standards, it certainly makes Bobby Jones' 1923 U.S. Open playoff victory, played in less than three hours, appear mythical. Why then, with so many modern advantages, is today's pace of play so slow?

In my opinion, it is a combination of factors. First, average golfers spend way too much time looking for the yardage markers, when in reality they are usually fortunate just to hit a green! Perhaps we have given them too much on-course information (i.e., yardage books, pin sheets, marked sprinkler heads, tee signs, et cetera, ad nauseam)?

Some claim the influence of the methodical Tour professional contributes to slow play, as generations of golfers have now grown up watching them play lengthy rounds and do not know that the three hour round is even possible. Certainly, it's an interesting point. Or, could slow play today be related to modern golf course architecture? Let's look at how designers can influence "pace of play" and you be the judge.

Routing

The single most important aspect of each golf course may be the time spent routing it. Many projects today are dependent on real estate to finance the golf course and thus incorporate road crossings and linear routings to create development frontage. The core, intact golf course is somewhat rare today. Certainly, where possible, minimizing the green to tee distance is favored. To achieve this, it is preferred to route the golf course first or at least in conjunction with the overall land use plan. There is no reason why we cannot build a first-class golf course which also satisfies the development demands of the present.

Bunkers

Deep fairway bunkers are out, and strategic, traditional-style bunkering is in. Strategically placed bunkers do not force the player to put the ball in the air, thus allowing the high-handicappers to play around the bunkers. Strategic design emphasizes that bunkers placed on one side of the playing area reward the boldly placed shot while affording the player with less ability to play away from the hazard. Compared to penal bunkering schemes, pace of play in strategic schemes is certainly increased, especially as a well-designed strategic hole requires less bunkering.

Large bunkers really slow down play because of the increased time it takes to rake the sand, and long linear shapes or clusters can achieve the same purpose as one large bunker. The architect must provide more than one access point, as too many bunkers only have one way in and one way out. The selection and quality of bunker sand is also important. Firm playing bunkers are preferred and play faster than soft, fluffy sand which often times results in buried lies—a real detriment to slow play.

Tees

Strategic design should dictate tee placement while not unduly penalizing or forcing a player to carry hazards. Properly placed tees and a number of teeing area options are favored. Unfortunately, too many players challenge the course from the wrong tee markers, perhaps the biggest contributors to slow play. Whatever happened to the Scottish custom of requesting permission to play the Medal (back) tees?

There are other factors that influence pace of play, in particular, daily course set-up and proper delineation of hazards. In the daily course set-up, the superintendent should consider weather conditions and the anticipated number of rounds. On heavy play days, minimize forced carries and do not tuck the pins.

Proper delineation of hazards and marking the golf course can also speed up pace of play. As my close friend and mentor Pete Dye once told me, create a hazard so the player is either in play or out, anything in between slows down play.

Finally, Bob Jones, well known for his no-nonsense style of play, left us with the following subtle anecdote to illustrate his feelings on architecture and pace of play:

> A lawyer went to extraordinary lengths to defend his client who was thereafter convicted anyway. The trial had been long and drawn out, lasting nearly a month and the lawyer had made quite a lot of noise and stormed eloquently in his argument. Meeting a brother lawyer on the street a few days later the case came up in discussion, and the lawyer asked his friend what he thought of his conduct at the trial. His friend replied: 'Well, I think you could have reached the same result with a whole lot less effort.'

~

Editor's Note
Crenshaw and Short Par-3s

If there is one depressing legacy of 1960's golf architecture, it's the disappearance of character and variety in our modern courses. In desperate marketing attempts to lengthen courses to 7,000 yards, as if that is some sort of mark of greatness, two types of holes have been forfeited: the drive-and-pitch par-4, and the short par-3. Thanks to a small group of modern designers (Mr. Dye and Messrs. Weiskopf and Morrish in particular), the short par- 4 is making a comeback.

However, the short par-3 has yet to recover from the "Dark Ages of Design," as some have called it. Ben Crenshaw, who understands and appreciates golf better than any great player since Bobby Jones, raises this point in the following essay, "The Short Par-3."

Mr. Crenshaw's fascination with architecture began at the age of sixteen when he left his homestate of Texas and played in the United States Junior Amateur at The Country Club in Brookline, Massachusetts. It was the first time Mr. Crenshaw had been exposed to traditional architecture and it was the beginning of his lifelong passion for the history of the game. Since then Mr. Crenshaw has compiled one of the finest private golf book collections in the world and has written numerous essays on all subjects of the game. Along the way, he has compiled a brilliant record as a player, winning the 1984 and 1995 Masters along with 19 other events on the PGA Tour.

With the 1995 unveiling of Sand Hills Golf Club, Mr. Crenshaw and his architecture partner, Bill Coore, introduced perhaps the most unique new golf course since the work of their mentors from the "Golden Age" of architecture.

G.S.

~

The Short Par-3

by Ben Crenshaw

In this era of obscene power, the likes of which the game has never witnessed, why not strive to induce a little fun into the mix and at the same time present a true test of delicacy and accuracy? Since this idea is not a new one, and it is certainly an idea that is, in effect, diametrically opposed to what seems to be in vogue today, allow me to give you a few examples of short par-3s that have always been fun to play and study:

#10 Pine Valley
#6 National Golf Links
#9 Whitemarsh Valley
#13 Merion
#7 Royal Melbourne
#7 Pebble Beach
#15 Cypress Point
#8 Royal Troon
#10 Chicago Golf Club
#12 Augusta National
#15 Kingston Heath

There are a number of reasons why these holes were listed for the sake of this brief discussion: (1) they possess an extraordinary shot value; (2) they offer a tight target set off by impressive and engulfing hazards in the form of water, deep or immediate bunkering, or stern green contouring, which makes the effective target even smaller; and (3) the length of these holes, God forbid, should be in everyone's range!

The length of the holes above, as one may deduce, is of the 150-yard and under variety. (What constituted a "pitch" in yesteryear was any shot of this length.) But this type of hole is a thrill for everyone, and usually elicits high drama for the tangible possibilities of scoring "2"—and anything upwards. Par-3s of this type call for proper execution, nerve, and bravery. Not only does this sort of hole require accuracy, but the stroke must be of

Photo by Geoff Shackelford *(Coore and Crenshaw)*

THE PAR-3 SEVENTEENTH AT SAND HILLS GOLF CLUB, MULLEN, NEBRASKA BY COORE AND CRENSHAW. ONE OF THE MOST EXCITING PAR-3'S YOU WILL EVER FIND. VIEW IS FROM THE 100-YARD MIDDLE TEE. PLAYS 146 YARDS FROM THE BACK TEE (TO THE RIGHT AND REAR OF THIS VIEW).

proper strength. And strength, in these cases, can be described in two ways: the proper length being the physical requirement; while having enough strength in the mental department to possess the control and authority over the ball which these types of holes demand.

I do not mean to imply that short par-3s do not exist anymore, though its type is not frequently attempted by many architects today. But quite selfishly, I would enjoy seeing more of them, for it's one of the many ways to check unbridled power, and occasionally, make those long hitter's knees tremble.

~

Editor's Note
Klein and Big Business

Throughout this book an effort has been made to provide a variety of perspectives on golf architecture. There has also been an attempt to celebrate the work of the "masters," and in this section we have the opportunity to reflect and comment on the evolution of design since the era when many of the essays in Parts I through IV were written. One of our true experts on architecture, Bradley S. Klein, has chosen to come right out and state exactly where golf architecture is today.

The Architecture Editor of *Golfweek*, where he runs that publication's national golf course rating system "America's Best," Mr. Klein has spent thousands of hours talking to an array of modern architects and knows the business as well as anyone. In "When Golf Design Becomes Big Business," he takes a strong stance in distinguishing between those who love the art of architecture and those who are in it merely for the money.

In 1997 Bradley Klein published a collection of golf essays, *Rough Meditations*, and is a frequent lecturer at industry and golf association meetings. In between stints as a PGA Tour caddie, he earned a Ph.D. in political science and now serves as assistant professor of government and international relations at Clark University in Massachusetts.

G.S.

~

When Golf Design Becomes Big Business

by Bradley S. Klein

Ask most golf course architects these days and they'll tell you the toughest part of the job. Designing 440-yard par-4s for players who regularly drive the ball 280? Hiding those cart paths so that golfers don't see wall-to-wall pavement? Negotiating with environmental agencies? Wrong on all counts. For the vast majority of designers, the hardest work is scrambling for plum assignments—or for any work at all.

Sure there are plenty of jobs out there. By industry estimates, some 300 new courses will come on line in 1997, a number that was only surpassed in the mid-1960s, when 350- 450 new layouts were opening annually. But there are many more designers than ever before, vying for that work. The prestigious American Society of Golf Course Architects now has a membership of 128. Back in 1966, it was only 29. And the ASGCA's ranks today only include about half of the working design firms in the country.

It seems that every other PGA pro and his caddie is getting into the design act. No sooner do they win a Quad Cities Open than they become an expert on linksland golf. After winning the Tour's 1996 money crown (and the 1996 British Open), Tom Lehman announced that he was cutting back on his Monday schedule of exhibitions in order to devote more time to his burgeoning design practice. Gee, maybe it's also possible to become a golf pro by practicing once a week.

Why shouldn't everybody try getting into the act? The fees—often approaching $1 million—sure sound impressive. The truth is, that's a number only the very elite get, and usually it's for overseas jobs. Most design fees are a quarter of that, and whatever the listed price, a lot of heavy discounting goes on by way of back-room bargaining.

What's the motive to hire a name? Some reputable accountants have figured that having a marquee name affixed to a golf property can boost the per lot retail price by as much as $50,000. It can also add $20–30 per round in terms of green fee—if the public is foolish enough to believe that having a name on the scorecard makes a difference in the golf course. What owners have found out, actually, is that having a big name pro lined up with a property will draw some early interest from the public and the media. But golfers aren't so gullible to sustain the charade for long. If the course is good, they'll return. If not, they'll stay away in droves.

Besides an economic motive to hire a big gun, there's the all-too common schmooze factor. Given the kind of heavy hitters often involved in golf course development, they want to feel like they're important and so they want to associate with big-name people. It massages their ego, impresses potential investors, and makes them feel like they have indeed earned their own lifestyle of the rich and famous.

To some extent, designers have internalized these "show biz" values. They arrive on the job in satin gold capes and travel with a fawning entourage—along with a bottle of designer water in hand. Then they wow their audience with flamboyant talk of the project being a "signature design."

It has become the most meaningless phrase in golf course architecture. Today, "signature design" refers to a famous golf pro's endorsement on the back of an inflated six-figure check for three photo opportunities, a cocktail party with the first 50 lot owners, and a flashy opening day gala, replete with a drive off the first tee—"hey, which way does the hole go?"

It isn't enough for a designer to have worked on the course. Now it has to be emphasized—like "real cheese flavoring"—that so-and-so actually devoted his time to it and spent four—count 'em, 4—site visits inspecting what turns out to be the work done by some low-paid assistant.

One golfing great who shall remain nameless is legendary for his site visits to his many signature designs—not one of which, it must be said, has registered the slightest tremor on the Richter scale of any regional golf market. He climbs up on a pile of dirt, rolls up a set of blueprints in his hands, and peers out in the fashion of Moses on the Mount while a pliant video crew tapes everything for history. No doubt the image will appear on the cover of a glossy brochure, replete with some fill-in-the-blank canned quotes about how "God decreed this land for a world-class golf course and I'm thankful for this opportunity to make the TPC at Lumbago Bay the finest of its kind."

Design shops today run the gamut, from mom and pop stores to major corporate undertakings encased in steel and glass bank buildings. You know you've run into a really big firm when the phone tree you hear upon calling into the office offers twenty-five nasally intoned options, each one for another assistant to the person you need to reach.

Many architects retain staff photographers to keep the public supplied with snazzy images and magazine-quality transparencies. They also regularly hire out work to public relations agents, ghost writers, and a retinue of lawyers and accountants. Architecture firms with full-time staffs larger than ten are common.

Care to figure out the overhead for office rental, computer equipment, travel, salaries and medical benefits? It takes three new projects a year just to meet the fixed costs. Small wonder that so many designers are consistently taking on new work as fast as they can. Given the vagaries of the business cycle, the uncertainties of funding, and the lengthy delays entailed in permitting, one never knows which projects will actually pan out—and pay up.

Many big-name designers spend all their time chasing down new assignments (and bad-mouthing rivals competing for the same job). They leave the actual nuts and bolts to a design team—or to a group of recent graduates of a Landscape Architecture program who busy themselves in the back room on computer screens. Whatever the case, too many designers these days don't spend enough time in the field actually building on the ground. Or they don't get their first glimpse of a project until they look at a routing plan prepared by a design associate.

Some still do the work themselves, from A to Z. Among them (and this is by no means a complete list): Bill Coore and Ben Crenshaw, Tom Doak, Pete Dye, Ron Forse, Gil Hanse, Ken Kavanaugh, Stephen Kay, Ron Prichard, Rick Smith, Steve Smyers, Mike Stranz, and Bobby Weed. They build courses the old-fashioned way, by hand, through the love of their craft. They've studied the game, its traditions, its literature, and they've traveled widely in search of classical form. Too many designers today, however, are engaged in mere promotion—or in cashing in upon their marquee value, without proper attention to the artisanal nature of their profession.

To be sure, golf course architecture has always been something of big business. A century ago, Willie Park, Jr. converted two British Open titles into a trans-Atlantic empire that included club and ball manufacturing as well as course design. During the Golden Age of Golf Design in the 1920s, transplanted Scotsman Donald Ross parlayed his many skills into the leadership of the country's largest landscape construction operation, with as many as 3,000 workers under his employ and half a dozen supervisors, many of whom went on to enjoy distinguished careers on their own as course architects. Of the 413 courses now properly credited to him, Ross never visited a third of them, preferring instead to churn out plans for them from his office in Pinehurst. Another third he only visited once or twice, and so he devoted his full attention to but 135 or so of the total. Yet the undeniable consistency of the quality he turned out and the easily recognizable stylistic themes he invoked attest to the care of his work.

Can one say the same thing today? It was Robert Trent Jones, Sr. after the Second World War who realized that golf courses could be profitably turned out in assembly-line fashion. Trent ceaselessly promoted himself, and more than any other designer turned his craft into mere business. The result, though it did include some very fine layouts, was far too many mediocre projects—the result of over-extension. And yet that didn't stop all too many subsequent designers from emulating this peculiar form of business success. The strangest phenomenon of all is that of the big-name designer who claims to be selective, yet a close inspection of his annual work list reveals more new courses per year than Trent. How does he do it? Simple. Each course looks the same.

Trent's worldwide fame at least emerged on the basis of his

architectural skills. Not so for many later designers, who quickly saw that their worldwide fame could be converted into a profitable traffic in golf course design.

The price of all this is difficult to assess. At least two distinct trends are discernible. One we will call the *Show Biz Effect.* Here, the emphasis is on turning golf design into a theatrical event, with the course designer in the lead role. This produces wildly inflated design fees and contributes to a Broadway atmosphere in which extravagant costs are seen not as a problem but as a matter of prestige and a guarantor of quality. Flashy designs, massive earthmoving, and glitzy features like a $1 million waterfall or an artificial island green: it's all part of a crass marketing atmosphere, one in which hype and headlines drown out the more enduring values of good, solid strategy.

The other we will call *The Mass Production Effect.* Here the interest is on turning golf design into an assembly-line operation in which courses are regularly pumped out with little regard for the particular qualities of the land. The primary interest is to reduce the time devoted to each layout and to maximize efficiency by shipping out plans to a builder. This approach tends to reduce unit costs, but it turns golf course design into a cloning operation that too often gets mistaken for "style" when what's really going on is the reduction of the craft to its simplest functional elements.

There's no reason why golf pros can't become designers. It's just that the road is a lot longer and more difficult than many of them think. When it comes to golf course architecture, there's no replacement for a careful study of the classics.

Extensive travel abroad is needed, along with meticulous research into turfgrasses and soils and a relentless desire to see everything that's being built. It helps, as well, to remember that not all golfers are scratch players, and that a tournament is only held one week a year whereas real golfers have to live with the place the rest of the year. Most important of all, a designer has to be willing to work the land by hand.

That takes time. A song and dance it's not. Nor an assembly line operation. When golf becomes big business, course design suffers.

Glossary of Terms

Approach/Entrance—The area directly in front of the green where approach shots may land and roll to the putting surface. Most prominent on links courses where sandy soil drains well and the turf is firm. Standards for soft, green turf have virtually eliminated the well-designed approach from modern designs in the United States. Also, many Green Committees discourage firm approaches for fear that leaving them open might render a course too easy when in fact more skill is required to approach a green with a shot on the ground. Having playable approaches (dry and firm) also creates opportunities to have firm greens, a more ideal situation for encouraging shotmaking and strategic play.

Barranca—A Spanish term to describe any gully, ditch, or watercourse. Term is used to describe deep hazards at several courses in Spanish-language regions such as California.

Bunker—A flattish area of sand surrounded by embankments. Many of these types of hazards developed naturally on the oldest Scottish links, and serve as the primary tool for the golf architect today in designing strategy and interest into courses.

Cape (grass)—Grassy points or "fingers" that divide bunkers into different, small sections. Used most prominently by architects to interrupt the edges of bunkers for purposes of creating an irregular or natural look. Used in early years predominantly by Alister MacKenzie, George Thomas, Billy Bell, and occasionally A.W. Tillinghast. Utilized in the design of bunkers in the modern era by Robert Trent Jones, Dick Wilson, and others.

Cape (hole)—Describes a style of hole used by everyone from C.B. Macdonald to Pete Dye where a tee shot must carry over a diagonal body of water to a point or "head of land." The longer the carry a player makes on the first shot, the easier and shorter the next shot. Most prominent example is Mr. Macdonald's 5th at Mid-Ocean Club in Bermuda.

Carry—A forced shot to be played over some sort of obstacle, usually a hazard.

Classic Course—Description for any vintage course built before 1940. To be considered a "classic," a course does not have to be ranked in the Top 100 of any particular magazine ranking. Instead, it is generally defined as a fine course of historical and architectural interest.

Cross Bunkers—Hazards designed at any angle to the fairway, creating different options from the teeing ground. A common trait of "strategic" architecture because it creates a situation where the player has a choice as to the type of carry shot to be played from the tee. Usually, the longer the carry made by the player, the easier the next shot should be.

Dogleg—Term used to describe a hole or fairway with a slight or even sharp turn to the right or left. Earliest known use of this term was by *Golf Illustrated* in 1902, and later popularized by writer Horace Hutchison.

Eden—See High Hole.

Featherie—Golf ball used before the introduction of the gutta percha in 1848. Featheries were leather covered and stuffed with feathers.

The Golden Age of Golf Design—Designation used to describe the period of golf architecture from approximately 1911 to the late 1930s. Commenced with the construction of C.B. Macdonald's National Golf Links and ended during the depression with Perry Maxwell's work. Virtually all of the "classic" courses built in the United States and Europe were constructed during this time frame, and most of the "master" architects were productive during this period: C.B. Macdonald, Alister MacKenzie, Donald Ross, A.W. Tillinghast, William Flynn, H.S. Colt, C.H. Alison, Seth Raynor, and Walter Travis. Several amateur architects also created timeless courses during this period: Hugh Wilson (Merion); George Crump (Pine Valley); Jack Neville, Douglas Grant, and H. Chandler Egan (Pebble Beach); George C. Thomas Jr. (Riviera with Billy Bell); and Bobby Jones (August National in collaboration with MacKenzie).

Gorse—Spiny shrubs native to Europe, most especially Scotland and Ireland, which bloom with fragrant yellow flowers and black pods.

Green Committee—Name given to a group of members at most golf or country clubs who oversee course maintenance on behalf of the membership. Several articles in this book refer to committees because of their involvement in course design matters, much to the dismay of many architects. Several once prominent courses have been permanently altered or ruined by committees interested in leaving their mark on the design. Most commonly Green Committees have deservedly retained their reputations through the overplanting of trees, adding needless bunkers, removing significant bunkers, or lengthening the course. ("Greens" is the incorrect usage; "Green" refers to the entire course, whereas "Greens" only refers to the putting surfaces.)

Gutty—The primary type of ball used between ca. 1840 and 1900. Consists of a thin, tough cord made from the intestines of animals, usually sheep. Fell out of favor (with an endorsement from the sheep) when the more durable Haskell ball came into play around 1900.

Haskell Ball—Predecessor to the modern ball, developed as a less expensive, more durable alternative to the Gutty ball around 1900 with a rubber core as its primary difference. There was a great deal of controversy over the Haskell ball due to its longer flight. It was also ridiculed because it threatened the livelihood of many Scottish golf professionals (it was easier to manufacture in large quantities, thus eliminating the need for handmade construction by the pros.)

Hazards—A difficult obstacle placed on the golf course that may cause some danger to the player, for which relief is granted in certain circumstances. Types of hazards include bunkers, lakes, creeks, ditches, barrancas, waste areas, or dunes. Water hazards (red) and lateral water hazards (yellow) are defined by painted stakes and lines. The club cannot be grounded in this type of hazard. For more on hazards, how they are defined, and how they should be maintained, see essays in Parts III, IV, and V.

Heather—A low-growing Eurasian shrub developing in dense masses and having small evergreen leaves and clusters of small, bell-shaped pinkish-purple flowers. Predominantly found on the courses of Scotland and Ireland. Balls can be found and many times played from heather, whereas gorse usually calls for an unplayable lie drop.

High Hole (also referred to as Eden)—The par-3 11th hole on the Old Course at St. Andrews. Consists of a wide green fronted in the middle-right by a deep bunker and protected on the left corner by another bunker. Several architects copied the High or built par-3s based on its principles, including C.B. Macdonald, Seth Raynor, Charles Banks, Alister MacKenzie, and H.S. Colt.

Lay-up—Shot played short of a green or hazard, the result of a decision by the player.

Layout—Another description for a golf course. Can also refer to the routing or sequence of holes.

Links—A term recently misused by most American developers to connote a course on a treeless site. Links are actually areas of very sandy soil once occupied by the ocean, and basically can only be found in Scotland. Linksland consists of many small undulations and deep bunkers, both created by wind. Pebble Beach is not on linksland, St. Andrews is. Robert Hunter describes the essence of links in his book, *The Links*: "On the links the player has not only to deal with the formidable hazards, but also with countless little ones —those beautifully turfed, harmless-looking undulations which run through the fairways from tee to green. Terrain of that sort will yield superlative golf anywhere. . . The true links were moulded by divine hands. Linksland, the fine grasses, the wind-made bunkers that defy imitation, the exquisite contours that refuse to be sculptured by hand—all these were given lavishly by a divine dispensation to the British."

Master Architect—Term used throughout this book to describe the most important architects from years past. A master can be defined as an expert, and only in this book is it used to describe the true experts from the early days of architecture. Master architects would include, but are not limited to: Old Tom Morris, C.B. Macdonald, Alister MacKenzie, Donald Ross, and A.W. Tillinghast.

Modern Architecture—Describes any course or design work commenced after World War II. Robert Trent Jones is largely credited with ushering in the modern era. Architectural characteristics of the modern era include large greens, penal as opposed to strategic bunkering, elongated tees designed for modern mowing equipment, and sometimes massive earthmoving by large equipment.

One-Shotter—Another name for a par-3 hole.

Out of Bounds—Land defined as the area outside of the course, from which play cannot take place. Shots landing out of bounds are penalized by one stroke and require the shot to be replayed from its original starting point.

Penal (architecture)—Style of design that emphasizes punishment of poor shots and physical skill over mental skill. Robert Trent Jones actually wrote in *The Complete Golfer* (1957) that the architecture of the '20s fell into this penal pattern "which punishes the golfer for the slightest error." This is actually a gross misstatement. The courses built during the '20s were highlighted by more strategic designs than any other period of course design. It was the design work of the '40s and '50s which placed bunkers on the sides of fairways and in front of greens to punish stray shots, and reward the physically superior who could hit their ball longest and straightest. Strategic architecture aims to reward the well-played shot, while the player who hits a poor first shot must play a strong following shot. The difference is that the strategic school encourages recovery while penal architecture rarely allows for recovery.

The Philadelphia School of Design—Name given to the remarkable group of architects who knew each other in the Philadelphia, Pennsylvania area between 1900 and 1925. Each was a scratch or low handicap player, and all were actively involved in George Crump's Pine Valley and Hugh Wilson's Merion designs. A.W. Tillinghast, William Flynn, and George C. Thomas Jr. all branched out of the Philadelphia area and designed several prominent courses in the United States.

Punchbowl—A type of green most commonly used in the early days of golf architecture before irrigation systems became prevalent, when it was important for grass greens to retain moisture. The center of the green on a punchbowl is located in a hollow, with the edges banked so that well-hit shots presumably funnel down to the middle of the green.

Redan—The name of the par-3 15th hole at North Berwick's West Links in Scotland. The Redan has been frequently copied by several architects, most notably C.B. Macdonald, Seth Raynor, Charles Banks, and A.W. Tillinghast. Other architects such as Hugh Wilson, George Thomas, and Alister MacKenzie have built "modified Redans." For a full definition and explanation of the Redan, see C.B.

Macdonald and H.J. Whigham's article in Part IV.

Redesign—Describes work by a committee, superintendent, or architect to alter the design of a course without concern for the original intentions.

Restoration—Describes work by a committee, superintendent, or architect to bring back a course to its original condition and design intention.

Routing—The order, positioning, and placement of the holes on a golf course.

Shot Values—A commonly used term with a rather ambiguous definition, depending on who you ask. According to Ron Whitten, the term was first used by William Flynn in the late 1920s. *Golf Digest*, who has popularized the term with its biannual course ranking, asks its panelists to rate shot values with the following prerequisites: "How well does the collection of holes present various risks and rewards and test accuracy, length, and finesse without overemphasizing any one skill over the other two?" Unfortunately, this is often misinterpreted, leading to a celebration of courses with so-called perfect "balance" and "fairness." Perhaps part of the shot values definition may best be defined in the interpretation of "Strategic," below.

Strategic (architecture)—Style of design that emphasizes a thinking as well as a physical response from the player. Strategic architecture rewards those with a plan of action who successfully negotiate a hole. On a strategically designed course, hazards are usually placed diagonally and "risk/reward" opportunities are created. Bobby Jones explained it best in *Bobby Jones on Golf*: "There are two ways of widening the gap between a good tee shot and a bad one. One is to inflict a severe and immediate punishment upon the bad shot, to place its perpetrator in a bunker or in some other trouble demanding the sacrifice of a stroke in recovering; the other is to reward the good shot by making the second simpler in proportion to the excellence of the drive. The reward may be of any nature, but it is more commonly one of three; a better view of the green, an easier angle from which to attack a slope, or an open line of approach past guarding hazards. In this way, upon the long, well-placed drive—possibly the one that has dared an impressive bunker—is conferred the greatest benefit, but shots of less excellence are still left with the opportunity to recover by bringing off an exceptionally fine second. A course constructed with these principles in view must be interesting, because it will offer problems a man may attempt, according to his ability. It will never become hopeless for the duffer, nor fail to concern and interest the expert; and it will be found, like old St. Andrews, to become more delightful the more it is studied and played."

Tableland—Expression used throughout Macdonald and Whigham's essay in Part IV to describe the green on the Redan. Defined as a flat, elevated region; a plateau or mesa.

Tee or Teeing Ground—Level ground maintained at a low mowing height where the hole commences.

Three-Shotter—Another name for a par-5 hole.

Trap or Sand Trap—See Bunker.

Two-Shotter—Another name for a par-4 hole.

Bibliography and Golf Books of Interest

Bauer, Alec. Hazards, *Those Essential Elements in a Golf Course Without Which the Game Would be Tame and Uninteresting*. Chicago: Toby Rubovitis, 1913.

Christian, Frank, with Cal Brown. *Augusta National and The Masters*. Chelsea, Michigan: Sleeping Bear Press, 1996.

Colt, H.S. and C.H. Alison. *Some Essays on Golf Course Architecture*. Worcestershire: Grant Books, 1993. (Facsimile of 1920 edition).

Cornish, Geoffrey and Ronald Whitten. *The Architects of Golf*. New York: HarperCollins Publishers, 1993.

Darwin, Bernard. *The Golf Courses of the British Isles*. London: Duckworth and Co., 1910.

Darwin, Bernard. *Golf Between Two Wars*. London: Chatto and Windus, 1944. (Facsimile of the 1944 edition by The Classics of Golf, 1985).

Davies, Peter. *The Historical Dictionary of Golfing Terms*. New York: Michael Kesend Publishing, Ltd., 1992.

Davis, Martin. *The Greatest of Them All*. New York: The American Golfer, 1996.

Doak, Tom. *The Anatomy of a Golf Course*. New York: Lyons and Burford, 1992.

Doak, Tom. *The Confidential Guide to Golf Courses*. Chelsea, Michigan: Sleeping Bear Press, 1996.

Dye, Pete, with Mark Shaw. *Bury Me in a Pot Bunker*. Reading, Massachusetts: Addison Wesley Publishing Company, 1994.

Hawtree, Fred. *Colt and Co*. Oxford: Cambuc Archive, 1991.

Hunter, Robert. *The Links*. New York: Charles Scribner's Sons, 1926.

(Facsimile of 1927 edition by the United States Golf Association, 1994).

Hurdzan, Michael. *Golf Course Architecture*. Chelsea, Michigan: Sleeping Bear Press, 1996.

Jones, Robert Trent, with Larry Dennis. *Golf's Magnificent Challenge*. New York: McGraw-Hill and Sammis Publication, 1989.

Jones, Robert Tyre. *Golf is My Game*. New York: Doubleday, 1960.

Klein, Bradley S. *Rough Meditations*. Chelsea, Michigan: Sleeping Bear Press, 1997.

Kroeger, Robert. *The Golf Courses of Old Tom Morris*. Cincinnati, Ohio: Heritage Communications, 1995.

Low, John L. *Concerning Golf*. London: Hodder and Stoughton, 1903.

Macdonald, Charles Blair. *Scotland's Gift - Golf*. New York: Charles Scribner's Sons, 1928.

MacKenzie, Alister. *Golf Architecture*. London: Simpson, Marshall, Hamilton, Kent, and Co., 1920.

MacKenzie, Alister. *The Spirit of St. Andrews*. Chelsea, Michigan: Sleeping Bear Press, 1995.

Matthew, Sidney L. *Life and Times of Bobby Jones: Portrait of a Gentleman*. Chelsea, Michigan: Sleeping Bear Press, 1995.

Rice, Grantland. *The Bobby Jones Story*. Atlanta: Tupper and Love, 1953.

Ross, Donald J. *Golf Has Never Failed Me*. Chelsea, Michigan: Sleeping Bear Press, 1997.

Shackelford, Geoff. *The Captain: George C. Thomas Jr. and his Golf Architecture*. Chelsea, Michigan: Sleeping Bear Press, 1997.

Shackelford, Geoff. *The Riviera Country Club: A Definitive History*. Pacific Palisades, California: The Riviera Country Club, 1995.

Sutton, Martin. *The Book of the Links*. London: W.H. Smith and Sons, 1912.

Thomas, George C. *Golf Architecture in America, Its Strategy and Construction*. Los Angeles: Times Mirror Co., 1927. (Facsimile of 1927 edition by Sleeping Bear Press, 1997).

Tillinghast, A.W. *Cobble Valley Golf Yarns and Other Sketches* and *The Mutt*. Far Hills, New Jersey: United States Golf Association, 1995. (Facsimile of the 1913 edition).

Tillinghast, A.W. (edited and compiled by Robert S. Trebus, Richard C. Wolfe Jr. and Stuart F. Wolfe). *The Course Beautiful: A Collection of Original Articles and Photographs on Golf Course Design.* New Jersey: TreeWolf Productions, 1995.

Ward-Thomas, Pat, et al. *The World Atlas of Golf*. London: Mitchell Beazley Publishers Limited, 1976.

Wethered, H.N. and Tom Simpson. *The Architectural Side of Golf*. Worcestershire: Grant Books, 1995. (Facsimile of 1929 edition).

Golf Architecture Related Web Sites

American Society of Golf Course Architects: www.golfdesign.org

Coore, Bill and Ben Crenshaw: www.bencrenshaw.com

Doak, Tom and Renaissance Golf Design: www.xgolf.com/doakgolf

Golf Collector's Society: www.golfcollectors.com

Golf Course Builder's Association of America: www.gcbaa.org

Golf Course Superintendent's Association of America: www.gcsaa.org

Golfweb: www.golfweb.com

Hurdzan, Michael and Hurdzan/Fry Design:www.hurdzan.com

igolf: www.golfcourse.com

National Golf Foundation: www.ngf.org

Royal and Ancient Golf Club: www.randa.org

Royal Canadian Golf Association: www.rcga.org

St. Andrews Links Trust: www.standrews.org.uk

United States Golf Association: www.usga.org

USGA Green Section: www.usga.org/green